DISRUPTED JOURNEY

DISRUPTED JOURNEY

*Walking with Your Loved One
Through Chronic Pain
and Illness*

NATE BROOKS

P U B L I S H I N G
P.O. BOX 817 • PHILLIPSBURG • NEW JERSEY 08865-0817

© 2025 by Nate Brooks

All rights reserved. No part of this book may be reproduced, stored in a retrieval system, or transmitted in any form or by any means—electronic, mechanical, photocopy, recording, or otherwise—except for brief quotations for the purpose of review or comment, without the prior permission of the publisher, P&R Publishing Company, P.O. Box 817, Phillipsburg, New Jersey 08865-0817.

Unless otherwise indicated, Scripture quotations are from The Christian Standard Bible. Copyright © 2017 by Holman Bible Publishers. Used by permission. Christian Standard Bible® and CSB® are federally registered trademarks of Holman Bible Publishers, all rights reserved.

Scripture quotations marked (ESV) are from the ESV® Bible (The Holy Bible, English Standard Version®), copyright © 2001 by Crossway, a publishing ministry of Good News Publishers. Used by permission. All rights reserved.

Scripture quotations marked (NASB) are from the New American Standard Bible® (NASB), copyright © 1960, 1962, 1963, 1968, 1971, 1972, 1973, 1975, 1977 by The Lockman Foundation. Used by permission. www.Lockman.org

Scripture quotations marked (NLT) are from the Holy Bible, New Living Translation, copyright © 1996, 2004, 2015 by Tyndale House Foundation. Used by permission of Tyndale House Publishers, Inc., Carol Stream, Illinois 60188. All rights reserved.

Italics within Scripture quotations indicate emphasis added.

Printed in the United States of America

Library of Congress Cataloging-in-Publication Data

Names: Brooks, Nate, author.
Title: Disrupted journey : walking with your loved one through chronic pain and illness / Nate Brooks.
Description: Phillipsburg, New Jersey : P&R, [2025] | Summary: "When your loved one's life is wracked by illness, your life changes too. This honest, deeply personal book helps readers to biblically process their own upended lives, relationships, and spiritual walk"-- Provided by publisher.
Identifiers: LCCN 2024043150 | ISBN 9798887791098 (paperback) | ISBN 9798887791104 (epub)
Subjects: LCSH: Pain--Religious aspects--Christianity. | Suffering--Religious aspects--Christianity. | Chronically ill--Religious life.
Classification: LCC BV4909 .B755 2025 | DDC 248.8/6--dc23/eng/20250106
LC record available at https://lccn.loc.gov/2024043150

To my wife, Kate,
whose steadfastness in suffering I aspire to,

and

to Jeremy and Alicia Wright,
faithful friends, fellow travelers, sanity-keepers.

CONTENTS

Introduction   9

1. When Suffering Isn't a Season   15
2. I Didn't Sign Up for This   25
3. A Stranger in a Strange Land   37
4. God, Interrupted   47
5. We Are Dust   61
6. Renegotiating Relationships   75
7. Cloud of Witnesses   87
8. The End   101

   Acknowledgments   109
   Appendix A: For the Non-Christian Reader   111
   Appendix B: Sexual Intimacy and Chronic Pain and Illness   115
   Notes   119
   Further Resources   125

INTRODUCTION

I don't know the specific story that has led you to pick up this book, friend. I doubt that you ever expected to be holding a book on your place in the mystifying world of chronic pain and illness. I certainly never imagined I would write one. But the fact that this book is in your hands means that you and I have watched Plan A for our lives evaporate, replaced by Plan B or Plan C or some other letter terrifyingly deep in the alphabet.

I want to start by telling you I'm sorry. I'm sorry that this is the path you must walk. I'm sorry you have to watch your loved one suffer. I'm sorry that you suffer in a hundred often unseen ways as well.

One day a couple thousand years ago, Jesus was asked by a lawyer what he considered to be the most important commandment given by God. "Love God with all your heart and love your neighbor as yourself," he said. That sounds so simple, doesn't it? But we know from our experience that simple commands often prove to be the hardest of all to follow, even in the best of times. This book is a meditation on trying to faithfully live out those oh-so-simple-sounding commands when life veers far away from being the best of times. How do we love God when he in his providence has allowed life-altering pain and illness into our loved one's life? And how do we love our loved one well when they are wrestling with their whole world being turned upside down?

If you're there, my hope is to offer you encouragement through this little volume. Those who suffer from chronic pain and illness often express that they feel forgotten or unseen by those around them. I'm grateful that more resources are becoming available to support those whose bodies feel deeply the sting of the curse. But for every person whose life is crumbling due to chronic pain or illness, there is at least one other person who loves them and must wrestle too with the reality of their own lives turning out very differently than they expected. If your life has been changed and disrupted by the suffering of someone you love, this book is for you. I can't say I'm an expert on everything you've gone through and are going through. There are many whose lives are more difficult than mine. But I hope we can walk together for a little while on this path and encourage each other.

WATCHING MY OWN HOUSE BURN DOWN

I am by vocation a counselor and professor. I specialize in caring for individuals and families caught in cycles of abuse and trauma. As such, my life is often a front-row seat to the terrible evils that people suffer from and inflict on one another. I've often thought that counselors and firefighters have a lot in common—we run into burning buildings to help, then retire to the station once the task is done.

But this book doesn't come from that professional place. This book isn't the equivalent of a book by a firefighter on the methods of extinguishing residential blazes. It's a meditation from a firefighter who has watched his own house burn down and been unable to stop it.

Introduction

My wife Kate and I met at a tiny high school on the central coast of California. It took me ten years to ask her out, but once I did I quickly realized that I should have used that past decade quite differently. She was the best of everything I never knew I needed—daring, spunky, always on the edge of doing something just a bit crazy. She sang. She danced. She spoke her mind. Her love for Jesus radiated out from every fiber of her being.

We tied the knot on one excessively warm afternoon in June 2013. Little did we know that the defining two words for the next eleven years and counting would be *chronic pain*. Our descent into that world began just six months after that happy day, and we've never made it back out of the hole.

I don't always know how best to describe what's gone wrong. There are so many levels—levels that undoubtedly you experience as well.

I could talk about medical details, a path littered with all manner of doctors and medications and hopes raised and dashed over and over again. Gone are the days of running together, the lengthy hikes in the woods, the ordinary easy movement and touch that framed our lives before.

I could talk about rewriting every category of life as chronic issues entrenched and we had to surrender to a new reality over and over and over again. Gone are the piles of homeschool curricula and tidy budgets and any semblance of a "normal"-looking two-parent household.

I could talk about the dark nights of the soul when the things we thought we knew and understood about God and ourselves and good theology were pressed far beyond what we could have ever imagined. Gone is the uncluttered relationship with God where his rule means that things generally turn out okay and the standard of human life is happiness.

I could talk about the pummeling effect chronic pain and illness have on relationships, of well-meaning people (who seemingly ought to know better) insisting that greater faith or essential oils can set your life back to normal if you just would truly believe. Gone is the feeling of being understood, of having a normal life that most people can relate to.

I could tell you that the first prayer my two-year-old daughter uttered on her own was "God, Mommy feel better?" Or about the times I have had to explain to my sons' teachers that, no, their mother wasn't dying; our boys were just processing their fear that she might. Gone is my kids' innocence as they inhabit a world where they learn of debilitating pain before My Little Pony or Pokémon or the other stations along the way of growing up.

Chronic pain and illness are the backdrop for the movie of our life. They were there when we were newlyweds trying to figure out how to take two lives and blend them into one. They were there as we welcomed three kids into the world and lived in four states. They were there as we watched God take Kate's father home to be with him. They have wound their way through every event, every milestone, every day of our existence. And barring something unexpected, we have about forty-five more years to go.

THE FASTEST OR THE LASTEST

Writing a book on suffering is a daunting task. You may have drunk far deeper from the cup of suffering than I have. I marvel at your strength and how God upholds you. Or you may wonder if you've earned your place at the table. *Sure, we have our struggles, but this idea of entire-life-rewriting pain and illness is farther into the cave than we've stepped.* It's true that some of us have heavier burdens to carry than others. But at the end of the day, each of us whose spouse, child, parent, sibling, or friend is afflicted with chronic pain and illness carries burdens. We're a community of people trying to figure out how to live a life that's no longer Plan A and endure in love like Christ does for us.

My favorite sport is long-distance trail running. (Strange, I know.) Right now, the top athlete in the sport is Courtney Dauwalter. She's rewritten every record in the book, including setting the course record at the Ultra Trail du Mont Blanc, a 106-mile race, by over an hour. (That's the equivalent of a team winning the Super Bowl 43–8.) For all her athletic achievements, I find her view of other runners even more impressive. She often talks in interviews about how she's not convinced she's the most impressive athlete in the field. After breaking the Tahoe Rim course record, she noted that, for her, "the best part of it all, I think, [is] cheering people in. We all cover the same trails. It doesn't matter what pace you did; everyone did 205 miles out there."[1]

I've found Dauwalter's advice helpful in so many ways as I meet new friends whose lives have been disrupted by a loved one's diagnosis of chronic pain and illness. There's no "fastest or lastest" in the world of suffering. We all have our unique struggles and challenges. Wherever you are on the road of learning to rewrite your life, my hope is that this book meets you.

FAMILY STORIES AND FAMILY PRIVACY

Before we turn to the first chapter, I do need to say one more thing. This book is my book, interwoven with parts of my story. It's not my wife's story. She'll float in and out of the pages as a prominent character, and I'll talk about some of what's happened to her.

Introduction

I've chosen not to share many details about what exactly has gone wrong physically for her. Her story involves the sudden onset of debilitating health issues whose origins have never been understood as well as medical interventions that did significant, permanent damage for which there is no cure. But the specifics are her story and hers to hold. It's not my place to share them in a book that the whole world can read. I know you likely face this tug-of-war as well in your own community—how much do we say and to whom?

I appreciate your willingness to give grace as I walk the tightrope of giving enough detail to be real yet not so much detail as to transgress wise family privacy. Kate is a counselor too, and she has read and approved everything in this book. In many places she's helped me better describe her and my experiences. We both want our experiences on the road we've walked to be used by God to encourage others navigating the rocky paths of chronic pain and illness.

As you turn the page and begin chapter 1, know that I'm praying for you. Your journey is one you never expected to set out on, but the way your faith and love compels you on is amazing.

1

WHEN SUFFERING ISN'T A SEASON

I WISH YOU COULD share my view with me as I work on this little book. We live on a heavily wooded lot, and it's fall. As a Californian transplant to the East Coast, I've only recently come to experience how lush green trees can be swallowed up in just a few days' time by the fiery beauty of thousands upon thousands of leaves spending their last few days of life beaming forth striking yellows and reds and every color in between. Fall in California rarely lasts more than a few days. Blink and you'll miss it. But here in the Carolinas, I've come to appreciate the varied seasons offered by our new home.

Fall turns into winter, those same trees bundled up tightly against the brisk temperatures awaiting the return of some warmth to stir them. Winter is crisp and clean, and then it is followed by the rain and storms and beauty of a Carolina spring. Trees stir, the air warms, new growth emerges. Eventually new growth matures, and the hot stickiness of summer begins its reign. The whine of cicadas keeps watch over my kids as they splash in the watering hole that collects in the backyard stream's lazy meandering.

Seasons come and seasons go. Each has something to complain about; each has much to be cherished. When I'm shivering and scraping ice off my windshield, I can know that sooner or later the layer of frost will be replaced with fresh warmth.

I don't know when we decided that *season* was the best word to attach to our experience of suffering. Do a quick search and you'll come back with an armload of books that aim to comfort you, equip you, and even prepare you for "seasons of suffering." The prayers that spill out of relationships ask God to "comfort and keep my brother (or my sister) as they walk through this season of suffering." And truly there are kinds of suffering that are seasons. We walk through the valley of the shadow of death and emerge out the other side.

But there are other kinds of suffering, other sadnesses, whose paths do not ever emerge from that dark valley. Each step is another step into suffering, and—though there may be times when the road is just a bit better—the road never finds its way out of the dismal swamp. So long as breath fills your lungs, there is no hope that the season will change. Winter is here, and it is not leaving. Here in this place, suffering isn't a season. It's become your life's climate.

FOR EVERYTHING THERE IS A SEASON?

God has left us more than a few mysteries in his Word, and one of those is who penned the book of Ecclesiastes. He signed off on his book as "Quoleth," which translates as "the Teacher."

Tradition and quite a few clues scattered throughout the book point to King Solomon as its author, but we aren't completely sure. Regardless of which ancient writer handed his wisdom down to us, the Teacher paints a picture of life that leaves us feeling uncomfortable. His opening words certainly set a mood: "'Absolute futility,' says the Teacher. 'Absolute futility. Everything is futile'" (Eccl. 1:2).

Some twelve chapters later, there hasn't been a great deal of movement in the Teacher's view of reality. He's explored everything a human being could hope to indulge himself or herself in, and yet when he drops his conclusion he's in the same place he began: "'Absolute futility,' says the Teacher. 'Everything is futile'" (Eccl. 12:8).

I don't know about you, but I find his perspective on life unnerving. Even more troubling is that the Bible calls him a "wise man" who "sought to find delightful sayings and write words of truth accurately" (Eccl. 12:9–10). The Teacher's not an optimist when it comes to surveying the kinds of lives that are available to human beings. He's tasted all the joys, and he ends his life telling anyone who will listen that his treasure trove of happiness cannot undo the emptiness of life.

The futility of life is the expectation of the Teacher. Left with two choices, instead of ending up with "rage, rage against the dying of the light,"[1] he says, "Remember your Creator in the days of your youth: Before the days of adversity come, and the years approach when you will say, 'I have no delight in them'" (Eccl. 12:1). There's a certainty, a finality, to the Teacher's words. The years will come when adversity piles up so high that you'll say, "I have no delight in them anymore."

It's easy to forget these words when life is full of happiness. There's a lot of things in life that bring joy. Good food, family, ministry, athletics, friends, nature, marriage, vocation—all are delights for our enjoyment. But the Teacher wants us to remember that even in the highest of all joy, days of adversity are coming. He's so sure of this that he wants us to make sure we understand that life is not a grand story in which things are always working from sadness to happiness, from brokenness to wholeness, from dark to light.

> For everything there is a season, and a time for every matter under heaven:
>> a time to be born, and a time to die;
>> a time to plant, and a time to pluck up what is planted;
>> a time to kill, and a time to heal;
>> a time to break down, and a time to build up;
>> a time to weep, and a time to laugh;
>> a time to mourn, and a time to dance. (Eccl. 3:1–4 ESV)

Maybe it's from this passage that we picked up on the idea that suffering is supposed to be a season. After all, the Teacher says there's a season for everything under heaven. There's a time to mourn and a time to dance. There's a time to weep and a time to laugh. Bad things are replaced by good things. See?

But as much as we may wish this to be the case, it's simply not what the Teacher would have us remember. Because for every line that moves from sorrow to joy, there's a line that moves the opposite way. There is "a time to search and a time to count as lost; a time to keep and a time to throw away . . . a time to love and a time to hate" (Eccl. 3:6, 8).

Every line of the Teacher's words is true. There is a time for mourning and a time for dancing. But his point isn't that mourning is *replaced* by dancing. The time of breaking down doesn't automatically blossom into a time of building up. These seasons aren't sequential, a promise that things are getting better. Sometimes they will. But for every sorrow that turns into a joyful reel, there will be love that will fall away into its opposite.

We may be tempted to look at this passage and say, "Well, we know that our ultimate destination is in heaven, so *all* suffering truly is just a season." And I certainly don't disagree with that. Indeed, the Teacher is really quite insistent that we remember God in the days of our youth because when all is said and done "the spirit returns to God who gave it" (Eccl. 12:7). But that's not what we typically mean when we talk in church or with friends about suffering being a season. We mean that this trouble will pass and we'll be able to go back to living a generally happy life here on earth.

That's why the Teacher's words are so disquieting. Someone who speaks of absolute futility doesn't sound like he expects life to be generally happy. There's a finality to his expectation that human life terminates in deep suffering. Even worse, when we start searching the other pages of Scripture, we find that this kind of thinking isn't limited to an author we can't quite identify with 100 percent certainty and who wrote a very long time ago.

Jesus assures his disciples, "You will have suffering in this world" (John 16:33). Paul begs God to remove his "thorn in the flesh," which makes his life so miserable that he names it a "messenger of Satan to torment me" (2 Cor. 12:7). Elsewhere Paul reminds the Roman Christians that God's creation is "subjected to futility" and "groan[s] together with labor pains." Every reader of that letter would look down at their hands and bodies and realize that they are part of that groaning creation, living in enfleshed futility as decaying nerves and tendons and gray matter cry out, waiting for "the redemption of our bodies" (Rom. 8:20, 22, 23).

God's words to us don't set the expectation that suffering is anything other than what we should expect on earth. But if I'm honest, suffering isn't my default expectation. I don't know if you're like me, but I read what I've written above and my heart starts to churn. *No. No. Yes, that's in the Bible, but we've moved past the days when that kind of suffering was normal. We have advanced medicine. We're more enlightened now. Things should be better.* But these expectations that suffering will be merely seasonal are born out of an environment in which prosperity, tranquility, and ease are the expected norm of life. Sure, suffering is real, but give it enough time and the medicine will work, the shivering frosts of winter will burst out into buds and blossoms in the warmth of spring. Just hang in there; just keep going. Because it will get better.

LIFE IN THE CLIMATE OF SUFFERING

Chronic pain and illness don't work that way, do they? They are, after all, chronic. If you're holding this book, you know just as surely as I do the ever-present hope of just one more doctor's appointment. *Maybe*, just *maybe*, this doctor, this procedure, this test, this claims-have-not-been-evaluated-by-the-FDA set of pills will prove to be *the* answer. Surely this must be the missing piece of the puzzle, because puzzles always have all their pieces and suffering is just a season and must fade.

But sometimes there's just no other puzzle piece that can be found. In C. S. Lewis's *The Lion, the Witch, and the Wardrobe*, little Lucy gasps when the fawn Tumnus sadly describes his land as one where it's "always winter and never Christmas" under the cruel reign of the White Witch.[2] But life in the land of chronic pain and illness moves one step beyond that grim, frosty reality. Even when the beautiful day of Christmas happens—a short, brilliant reprieve from symptoms, a special event or trip, or the delight of a virtual call with a friend who just gets it—it always goes back to being winter. It's Narnia at the North Pole, a world where the snow and the frost and the ice just *are*.

Here, suffering isn't a season; it's the climate. And—as one friend quipped to me—so often, as with our climate today, things just seem to be getting worse. A sudden downturn becomes the new normal. The hours of pain lengthen, and the fierceness of pain deepens. An accident or injury maims further. "Surely it'll get better" turns to "I hope it will get better," which then turns to what we thought was unsustainable becoming the new normal.

THE EMOTIONAL PROSPERITY GOSPEL

I come from a theological tradition that has long recognized the folly and danger of the prosperity gospel. Our radar is well attuned to seeing through preachers living gilded lives, promising that God will throw open the storehouses of heavenly wealth or success or power in exchange for money given in faith. But while we've chased away the economic prosperity gospel from the front door with an eye roll and rightly interpreted Bible passages, far too often we've let in his cousin through the back door. We know enough to reject a gospel that proclaims faith begets wealth. We're far more susceptible to a gospel that believes faith begets unruffled contentment. That gospel, the emotional prosperity gospel, flourishes when we believe that deep, pervasive, unending suffering is an imposition into the normal life of relative ease and health.

Our history as a species helps us realize just how untrue the emotional prosperity gospel is. God gave us the first glimpse of the gospel right after Adam and Eve plucked the forbidden fruit from the Tree of the Knowledge of Good and Evil. After explaining the terrible reality of what their new habitat and life would look like—a life that would end with their returning to the dust from which they were made—God promised that one day a descendant from the woman would crush the head of the devil who deceived them (Gen. 3:15). This gospel, this good news, has been around as long as that terrible curse has governed the boundaries of where we live our lives. And while it has been a source of hope and salvation, it has not turned human life into a space free of pervasive trouble.

For most of human history, chronic pain and suffering lurked just around the corner. Have you ever stopped and wondered how many of Abraham's shepherds tore an ACL running down a flighty sheep? Or how many of David's warriors felt the crunch of bone during a routine training exercise gone wrong? Or how many mothers didn't recognize their own bodies after childbirth (if they survived it)? In the expansive ages without surgical interventions, such maladies were permanent with no hope of recovery. The popping of a ligament often sentenced a person to an entirely different life from the one they had known before. One wrong turn on a knee, one fall down a staircase, and nothing would ever be the same.

The Scriptures show us a picture of one such chronic pain sufferer. Little Mephibosheth, the five-year-old son of Prince Jonathan, was snatched up by one of his nurses upon hearing that his father and grandfather, King Saul, had been killed by the Philistines in battle. In the commotion and hurry, Mephibosheth fell from her arms, gravely injuring both of his feet. He never recovered from his injury, living the rest of his days as a cripple.

Chronic pain and illness quickly bring us back to a reality that we tend to forget in our age of much more advanced medicine. When all is said and done, we are not the masters of our fate or the captains of our souls. Many diseases and conditions of the past have been driven into obscurity by antibiotics and vaccinations and surgery. And yet our modern advances cannot entirely outrun the truths that the Teacher spoke long, long ago. Our default is suffering, "absolute futility," as our bodies wait with groaning for redemption.

It's easy to forget this when so many babies have had holes in their hearts repaired, so many broken vertebrae have been fused, and so many tumors have been removed. Our hearts cry out, "It shouldn't be like this!" But we have to realize that those cries are a longing for Eden, the place where there was no chronic pain or illness, and not a realistic picture of what life on a cursed earth is expected to be like. I am so grateful that some of my friends have been spared a dark descent into the world of chronic pain and illness because of a doctor's knowledge and skill. But they are the exception and not the rule. Throughout our history, more humans haven't recovered than have recovered. And when my heart cries out, "It's not fair!" these words emerge from the emotional prosperity gospel, the gospel that leads me to believe that ease and happiness and tranquility and health are supposed to be my default life experience right now. Yes, God steadies us in the storm. But no, his steadiness does not set everything aright. It's not that time yet.

The emotional prosperity gospel also contributes to some of the terribly unhelpful comments made to sufferers of chronic pain and illness and to their families. Verses taken as promises that are not promises, unsolicited medical advice, trite Christian phrases, unwarranted and unkind assumptions, and countless other well-intended but sorrow-producing things often illustrate how, at least in the world of health, those around us often live in a different climate than the one we do. The emotional prosperity gospel is able to grow in a climate where deep medical suffering is not the norm, at least not until you reach an age when the body is expected to begin wearing out. People often struggle to understand just how all-encompassing the life disruption caused by chronic pain and illness can be, and that can be incredibly isolating.

Thankfully a real gospel is out there, a gospel that makes the emotional prosperity gospel seem like a cheap trinket. It, after all, is a story of God himself stepping from heaven into this world of absolute futility. He arrives. He shows us his glory. He is crucified. He rises again. He departs to prepare an eternal future place for us. He sends his Spirit to transform us and strengthen us until we go to be with him. The real gospel is not aloof from or ignorant of all the sorrows and pains we experience. It doesn't erase our pain, but it offers strength for weary hands and comfort for grieving hearts. You may have questions about this true gospel, questions that may have emerged only after you have come face-to-face with the destructive power of chronic pain and illness. If so, that's okay. We'll talk more about this in chapter 4. Until then, watch and see how God meets you throughout the next chapters. Your great suffering requires a great hope, and Jesus is the great hope of the world.

2

I DIDN'T SIGN UP FOR THIS

The world of chronic pain and illness is confusing, isn't it? It's like moving to a new city without a map. There are plenty of familiar sights. The same chain restaurants cluster around familiar-sounding hotels and highways. Steeples dot the skyline here and there, and traffic predictably piles up around commuting time. But everything's rearranged. The same elements are there, but if you take a right at the shopping mall, you now run into the park instead of the downtown. The elements of life are familiar, but it's like someone crammed them all into a box and shook them up for a while.

A loved one's diagnosis (or trouble without diagnosis) doesn't remove us from the lives we used to live. My day still consists of teaching classes, running to the grocery store, helping my children learn to navigate life, washing dishes, scrounging up money to play tooth fairy, taking the truck to the mechanic, paying bills, planning holidays, and doing the thousand other things that weave together to form life. And yet none of these categories remains untouched by the health implosion that befell my wife.

Comedian-turned-author Cathy Crimmins helped me put words to this phenomenon in her book *Where Is the Mango Princess?* Crimmins's tax-lawyer husband suffered a gruesome traumatic brain injury in a boating accident in rural Canada. While he survived, the Alan who woke up from a coma was very different from the Alan whose brain had not been run over by a speedboat. (The book's odd title comes from a nonsensical question Alan asked over and over and over again during his stay in the hospital.) Cathy writes,

> Accidents divide things into the great Before and After. Here's how I see it: One day you and your family are hiking across a long, solid plain, when out of the sky comes a blazing meteor that just happens to hit one family member on the head. The meteor creates a huge rift in the landscape, dragging the unlucky one down to the bottom of the crevice it has made. You spend the next year on a rescue mission. . . . How do you even get him out? . . . It's not easy. The chasm between the old life and the new is wider than you think. You could fall into the darkness yourself, trying to jump across. And that damned crevice is always there, the bad-luck meteor stuck down inside it. You turn your back on it and go on, across that wide plain of life, again. But along the way you have to tell the improbable story of the meteor. You have to describe the big hole in the ground and the little holes it left behind. You dream about the time before the meteor came down without warning. . . . It is the beginning of a new and bewildering journey.[1]

Not all chronic pain and illness stories have a definable moment when everything changed. Often a diagnosis comes after a long period of frustrating and mysterious struggle, or there's never the clarity of a diagnosis—just the dull frustration of knowing that the body has changed and nobody can figure out why. But regardless of your journey's origin story, all of us can relate to there being a Before and an After. I have a Before wife and an After wife. You may have a Before child and an After child or—depending on your relation to the afflicted—a Before parent and an After parent. We all have Before lives and After lives, regardless of whether the region between the two is marked by a slow glacial descent or The Moment that will forever be seared in your memory.

It's not easy to build an After life. Do you plan on the After life being permanent? Is that giving up hope? Is it faithfully accepting a hard turn of providence? What do we keep? What must we give up? How do we navigate the new ways that we relate to each other, to the things we've lost, and to the things we've gained? And all this happens in the middle of a life that continues to march onward. You don't take a month off to rebuild your After life. You just have to adapt on the fly, not knowing what the next day or month or doctor's visit will bring and how you may have to rewrite the whole plan all over again.

"OUR PROBLEM," NOT "YOUR PROBLEM"

But before we go any farther, it's worth taking a moment to ask why any of this should matter to you at all. *Your* nerves aren't the ones crying out. *Your* body isn't the one that is shaking itself to pieces. *You* aren't the one who is breaking down. So why should your life be interrupted by someone else's pain? After all, there are people all over the place whose sorrows and troubles we don't take upon ourselves. If we tried to carry the burdens of the world, we'd fall to pieces, so why shouldn't we all simply saddle our own burdens and get on with life?

It didn't take God long to tell us that he's designed different kinds of relationships for us. After Adam finishes naming all the animals, he's dismayed that while there are two lions and two grasshoppers and two of everything else, there's only one of him. Having shown him his need for a partner, God causes Adam to fall into a deep sleep and creates another person equal to him in worth, in wisdom, in value. Adam sees her for the first time and bursts out into poetry, declaring with joy that "this one, at last, is bone of my bone and flesh of my flesh; this one will be called 'woman,' for she was taken from man" (Gen. 2:23).

The narrator in the book of Genesis wants to make sure we don't miss what just happened here. He interrupts the story to give us an important aside: "This is why a man leaves his father and mother and bonds with his wife, and they become one flesh" (Gen. 2:24). The relationship between a husband and wife is different from other relationships. I have many friends, but two become one in none of those relationships. While my wife and I are separate, autonomous persons, our hearts are knit together and intertwined in a way that's different from our relationships with other people. In a healthy marriage that functions as God intended, your spouse's victories are your victories, their sorrows are your sorrows, and their pain is your pain because two have become one in the covenant of marriage.

Parents and children also have a different kind of relationship than others. Parents are charged by God to showcase to their children what a life that is reconciled to God looks like (Deut. 6:6–7). And children are to honor their parents as their parents help them flourish (Eph. 6:1). God built our families to be collections of individuals, people whose relationships are woven together in a way not shared by others.

Perhaps you're reading this not as a relative of someone suffering from chronic pain and illness but as a friend or a fellow church member. One of the beautiful things about the body of Christ is that we become as family to one another. You and the suffering person you love may not share the same genetic stamp within the blood coursing through your veins, but you have become siblings because you've been adopted by God into his family. We are all blood brothers and blood sisters through our Savior's blood shed on the cross. To us, God gives instruction to "carry one another's burdens; in this way you will fulfill the law of Christ" (Gal. 6:2). God never designed us to simply shoulder our own burdens. Instead, we "rejoice with those who rejoice" and "weep with those who weep" (Rom. 12:15).

All three of these relationships—spouse, relative, and friend—involve promises that people make to each other before God, designed by God. When you married your spouse, had children, or joined a church body, you became part of them. The English poet John Donne beautifully captures our interconnectedness in his famous lines:

> No man is an island,
> entire of itself.
> Every man is a piece of the continent,
> a part of the main.
> If a clod be washed away by the sea,
> Europe is the less. . . .
> Any man's death diminishes me,
> because I am involved in mankind.
> And therefore never send to know

for whom the bell tolls,
it tolls for thee.[2]

If the pain suffered by someone within these relationships has little impact on your emotions and daily life, it should serve as a flashing light warning that you may be dangerously disconnected from them. I'm not talking about caregiver burnout, where you see yourself slowly fading into disconnection, ground into dust by pure exhaustion. Rather, I mean when you watch their hurt and your heart responds with a dismissive "That's your problem." There is no such thing as a "your problem." It's always an "our problem."

A few months after my wife's ill-fated surgery, we began to truly acknowledge that something was seriously wrong. My natural optimism that "things will be okay" proved ineffective at holding back the dam of reality. Suddenly I was staring at an After life, no longer able to pretend that we were just a few weeks away from returning to our happy and comfortable Before life. I entered a very dark place as this realization began to settle like black, sooty dust within my heart. Memories of that time are a blur, but I have several snapshots of me aggressively raking leaves in our acre-sized backyard, a yard that had been my wife's dream to own.

With each stroke of the rake, "I didn't sign up for this" marched its way across my mind. I didn't sign up for working two jobs to cover our medical bills and our kids' school tuition. I didn't sign up for her emotions being all over the place. I didn't sign up for getting paltry amounts of sleep every night. I didn't sign up for solo parenting most days. I didn't sign up for traveling to three doctor's appointments a week. And I certainly didn't sign up for having to rake this massive lawn all alone.

After a couple of months of this (and I'm sure they were

a couple of months where I was a miserable husband to live with), my reverie was suddenly snapped by a thought that I was instantly embarrassed hadn't occurred to me before. "Of course you did." This thought was unwelcome, but it wouldn't stop. "Of course you signed up for this. You stood in front of two hundred witnesses and promised to this woman and to God that you would love her 'for better, for worse, for richer, for poorer, in sickness, and in health.' You literally said the exact words that you would love her if illness consumed your lives."

When I said those words, I couldn't have imagined their gravity, or that I was writing checks my heart would later balk at cashing. But that's how most promises in life go. We promise, though we are unable to control what the cost of keeping those promises turns out to be. A man or woman joining the armed forces doesn't know what global events may arise in the course of his or her service. You bear or foster or adopt a child having no control over the course their life will take, not knowing if the road is joy or sorrow or a complicated blend of both. You decide to follow Jesus, not knowing what terrain that path will wind itself through across the next several decades of your life.

Years after Jesus ascended back to heaven, John Mark wrote one of the Gospels after interviewing the apostle Peter, who preserved a conversation between Jesus and two of his disciples. It reminds us that ignorance of the future doesn't negate the promises we make.

> James and John, the sons of Zebedee, approached him and said, "Teacher, we want you to do whatever we ask you."
> "What do you want me to do for you?" he asked them.
> They answered him, "Allow us to sit at your right and at your left in your glory."

Jesus said to them, "You don't know what you're asking. Are you able to drink the cup I drink or to be baptized with the baptism I am baptized with?"

"We are able," they told him.

Jesus said to them, "You will drink the cup I drink, and you will be baptized with the baptism I am baptized with." (Mark 10:35–39)

I wonder if James reflected back to this conversation as he sat in a dungeon years later, arrested by King Herod for preaching that Jesus was the Messiah who rose from the dead. I wonder how often his brother John considered the bargain they'd made after he watched James be run through with a sword, the first of Christ's twelve disciples to become a martyr, just twelve years after Christ ascended to heaven.

When we say, "I didn't sign up for this," we're often really saying, "I don't want this." Of course we don't want this. Our loved ones hate the suffering that's going on within their own bodies. They don't want this. Nobody wants to be here. And if I may be so bold, let me suggest that if anyone has the right to say, "I didn't sign up for this," it's the one whose body drew the short end of the straw—not you, the one who signed on to love them and sacrifice for them even if their body started breaking down far before you ever thought it would.

Like many people in my circles, I have an affinity for Tolkien's *The Lord of the Rings*. (Although I must say that I read the books *before* watching the movies.) Faced with resurgent evil and coming to realize the role he must play in its defeat, the young hobbit Frodo sighs to the old wizard Gandalf,

"I wish it need not have happened in my time," said Frodo.

"So do I," said Gandalf, "and so do all who live to see such times. But that is not for them to decide. All we have to decide is what to do with the time that is given us."³

The Lord of the Rings is far from being the only story with such a message. My two-year-old is far more captivated by princesses than by orcs. But even her fairy tales teach her that sometimes princesses face the reality that all is lost, sorrows abound, and all that is left to do is the next right thing.

Such stories feel safe when plastered on the screen or page, and especially when surrounded by inspirational music, but when they are rooted in our lives we are forced to come to terms with just how grim and bleak and gutting unending suffering is.

SCRIPTURE AND THE AFTER

One of my favorite things about the Bible is how unflinchingly real it is. Our Holy Book is full of terrible and unholy things. It's no stranger to the muck and the mire of what life is like under the curse. The Bible's full of real people's raw emotions as they try to wrap their minds around all kinds of troubles that befall them. The Bible shows us that good theology doesn't simply place a bandage with some colorful design over the top of deep heart wounds. Rather, it records just how dark a place God's followers may descend to. Listen to the confusion, the panic, the despair that weave their way through the following words:

> Why was I not stillborn;
> why didn't I die as I came from the womb?
> Why did the knees receive me,
> and why were there breasts for me to nurse?

> Now I would certainly be lying down in peace;
> I would be asleep.
> Then I would be at rest. (Job 3:11–13)

> I have had enough troubles,
> and my life is near Sheol.
> I am counted among those going down to the Pit.
> I am like a man without strength,
> abandoned among the dead.
> I am like the slain lying in the grave. (Ps. 88:3–5)

> I am deeply grieved to the point of death. (Matt. 26:38)

> We were completely overwhelmed—beyond our strength—so that we even despaired of life itself. Indeed, we felt that we had received the sentence of death. (2 Cor. 1:8–9)

If you have a moment, go back through those passages and highlight the intense phrases that pop off the page. Things like "I've had enough," "deeply grieved," and "completely overwhelmed." It's easy to gloss over the emotions of people long since dead, but each of these authors was a real flesh-and-blood person just the same as you and me. When they put quill to parchment, they didn't mince any words. They grabbed the strongest phrases you can grab and were happy to say, "Yes, 'I am like the slain lying in the grave' is the best way to describe my experience right now."

I don't know about you, but before I came face-to-face with lives being consumed with chronic pain and illness, these phrases seemed to be a bit on the dramatic or overstated side. That may not be your situation, especially if you grew up in an abusive or troubled environment. But for me, while I'd known sorrow, "I am like a man without strength, abandoned among the dead" was a few bridges beyond where I'd traveled on the trail of suffering. I developed a habit of anesthetizing these passages, draining the horror out of them so that they'd better match my experiences. They became poetic overstatements of trouble. But that's not how they're written. I just hadn't suffered enough yet to understand them.

But a few months or years into playing doctor's office chauffeur, bathroom scrubber, laundry folder, midnight trauma counselor, backyard leaf raker, insurance wrangler, lunch packer, masseuse, bill payer, faith supporter, child taxi driver, professor, diaper changer, budget balancer, griever, medical procedure investigator, wish fulfiller, school arranger, leaky sink fixer, knee bandager, off-key bedtime hymn singer, dinner cooker, and the thousand other roles that comprise every minute of every day, the phrase "I am like a man without strength, abandoned among the dead" starts feeling a little more apropos.

THE "BAD NEWS GOSPEL"

It's really good news for you and me that the Bible is true to life about what kinds of awful things can befall us and how they can affect us. Imagine for a minute if the Bible were only a happy book. Promises like "I will be with you always" would fall incredibly flat if all you ever saw in the Scriptures were people having radiant lives and joyful feelings. We would look into our lives and feel creeping up into our hearts a natural question: "God, you say you'll be with us always, but there's nobody whose experience looks like mine. How do I know that promise was actually for people like me?"

That would be a valid and just question. But it's not a question we have to wonder about with the Bible God has actually written us. A tremendous host of characters dot the pages of Scripture with their tears and their griefs and their sorrows. Even our Savior was a "man of sorrows" who was "acquainted with grief" (Isa. 53:3 ESV). In the words of American theologian B. B. Warfield, Jesus "[embraced] that whole series of painful emotions which runs from a consternation that is appalled dismay, through a despondency which is almost despair, to a sense of well-nigh complete desolation."[4] Jesus dreaded the cross and was distressed to the point that his perspiration drenched the ground as if he'd had a major artery severed (Luke 22:44). We aren't expected to stare at the way life has been shunted over onto a track we never expected to travel and go about skipping. Rather, we mourn from collateral damage as the cursed futility of the earth reaches up to strangle the life of the person we love.

This is the "bad news gospel." The Scriptures show us that our days may follow a heavy road, full of tears and calamity. There might not be any getting better this side of heaven. The burden might not be lifted. But the good news in the middle of this bad news is that when the words "I will never leave you or forsake you" fell from our Savior's lips, he had full knowledge of the pain that you are experiencing right now. God looks unflinchingly at human suffering—at your suffering—and isn't surprised by any of it.

3

A STRANGER IN A STRANGE LAND

I HAVE BEEN FASCINATED by space for as long as I can remember. This wonder was probably aided by my dad recording every episode of *Star Trek: The Next Generation* on VHS for endless rewatching long before streaming was even on the map. My science elective in college was astronomy, and even now I enjoy standing on my back porch or running country roads after dark and staring up at the night sky.

The images provided to us by the Hubble Space Telescope and its successor, the James Webb Space Telescope, reveal that space is both beautiful and violent. From Saturn's rings to the Andromeda Galaxy, the vast and unmatched beauty of God's creation takes my breath away. At the same time, other images betray the hostility of space. Astronomical event AT2021ehb is hardly a household name. Sitting over 250 million light-years from us, AT2021ehb is the chronicle of a star slowly being ripped apart by a massive black hole. Astronomers witness this star being stretched like a piece of taffy as the black hole robs it of its matter and mass. Eventually even light will fail to escape gravity's pull and the once brightly shining star will fade into blackness.

Of all the events in the night sky, AT2021ehb might serve as the best metaphor for the life of a family caught up in the world of chronic pain and illness. Life as you know it gets slowly stretched, devoured by the chronic-pain monster's seemingly insatiable appetite. Be it in the violent upheaval of a sudden diagnosis or the slow fade of ever-decreasing functionality, life as you know it gets drained of its mass and heat and light.

We can often feel helpless to stem the tide. That sense of helplessness in the face of such loss is not an easy burden to bear. Life as a chronic pain and illness family is often terribly unstable, tossed about by symptoms and procedures and treatments that are largely outside your control. In this chapter we turn to exploring these challenges and end by discussing ways to live with such loss and instability.

LOSING THE LIFE THAT YOU'D DESIGNED

I live in a neighborhood where no two houses look the same. Similarities can be traced across the rooflines and porches and layouts, but every house has its own unique spin on human habitation. Ours was described by our Realtor as "every Midwesterner's dream home" (which I think means it's far more functional than fashionable), while my neighbor's is a 1970s subterranean structure built directly into a hill—a hobbit house way before hobbits were cool. Each of these homes bears the stamp of its original owners, its design demonstrating what they valued in a living space.

As with this row of 1970s custom-built houses, you and I are also designers of our own lives. There are things in life that are outside our control, but we largely have the opportunity to pick how we live. Some families take in the subtle joys of an unhurried pace of life. Others pack their calendars like there's no tomorrow. Some save every penny for the future, while others enjoy the moment a little more. Some homes witness closer parenting, others a looser approach to raising children. The lane we drive in typically is the one that best represents our personalities, influences, and circumstances. We live how we do because, frankly, we *like* it.

If you were to rewind the tape and look at the life Kate and I built together in the first act of our lives, you probably wouldn't be that surprised. I worked a ministry job with a static 8–5 schedule, and Kate stayed home with our small children. The budget was tight as we lived off one early-career income, but life was full of walks and going to the park and all the simplicity that love and a lack of wealth produce. We started homeschooling when the time came, and our life revolved around our church community. We were typically among the first to arrive every Sunday and the last to leave. We invested financially in our church's progress. We had people over two or three times a week for fellowship and fun. Pick three words to describe us and you'd probably land on *open*, *available*, and *energetic*.

This first act of our life is the life that we wanted, the life that we designed together. But the second act looks nothing like it. The characters are the same, but the plot seems to have been ripped from an entirely different production.

Gone is the predictable 8–5 job, replaced by an ever-rotating schedule of teaching, getting to the week's doctor's appointments, and watching our youngest, who is still a toddler. There is no groove, no rhythm repeated week to week. Our kids attend public charter school alongside a thousand other residents of our town. After school each day they walk over to their fitness program to build muscles and get their wiggles out while I finish my workday. Giving generously has been replaced by working multiple jobs to cover ever-escalating medical bills. Kate works part-time as a counselor and an artist, providing both income and purpose in a way that doesn't overly tax her limited stores of energy. Community groups are well out of reach, and our primary ministry at church is to attend the worship service. Half the time we're late due to morning health challenges, and we'll often go more than a month without making it to church as an entire family. We're lucky to have one family over a quarter. Reach into your bag of words for this act and you'd probably choose the grim opposites of the first act: *surviving*, *isolated*, and *exhausted*.

The life we're living now in no way feels like it's *us*. Our desires, delights, and convictions haven't changed at all. We still long for the pattern of life that we had. Yet due to chronic pain and illness, we've become the hospitable family who has almost nobody over, the educators who outsource their children to others, and the church conversationalists who often don't even make it out their front door on a Sunday morning.

Now just to be clear, I don't think that the first act was a more faithful approach to life. It was one lane on a big highway of many different lanes of faithfulness. We found the lane that we enjoyed and were happy to drive in it with respect and appreciation for those who chose different lanes. But we *liked* our lane. And now we look at our lives like Moses looked around Midian after fleeing Egypt, declaring, "I [am] a stranger in a strange land" (Ex. 2:22 KJV).

You too have likely experienced this sense of alienation or dislocation from your own life. Whether this dislocation is confined to certain categories or is more whole-life like ours, there's something deeply unsettling and disquieting about constantly living a pattern of life that's different from what your heart desires. Chronic pain and illness begin to dictate your life to you, reducing your options and taking control over what your life is going to look like.

INSTABILITY

The unfortunate reality is that even when you've become a stranger in a strange land, you're likely going to have to uproot and move yet again. You settle, memorizing the streets and locations of things you'll need. You adapt to the new foods and culture of your adopted homeland. This is how we do childcare. This is how we do work. This is what meals look like. Here's what we do with the budget.

And then in one doctor's appointment, one sudden spike in symptoms, one plunge of the thermostat locking up the body—it all disappears. Your new country crumbles underneath you, and you must begin yet another trek to yet another strange land and begin building again.

One week we went to the doctor's office and they tripled my wife's physical therapy appointments. *Now how do we fit this into our family schedule?* we both thought. *And how do we fit it into the budget?* Rip, rip, rip went the blueprint. Another hasty rearranging of work hours, more cutting back on the activities that had come to provide some stability.

As you read this book, you may feel this sense of instability acutely. Life becomes tentative, tossed about at the mercy of white blood cell counts. A sudden drop in temperature or rise in humidity cancels all best-laid plans. Everything becomes a frustrating "maybe" as all plans must be written in pencil rather than pen.

This sense of instability can take a dark turn as well. Kate and I both find ourselves longing at times to know what the future holds, not for curiosity's sake but so that we can live life now in a way that will minimize future regrets. If Kate's going to get better, then we can hang on for dear life as long as we must. But if—and I shudder as I write this—the path is paralysis and early death, then that would significantly alter how we do life, spend money, and build memories now.

Chronic pain and illness thus beget both microscopic and macroscopic instability. You never know what kind of day you're waking up to, and you also don't know how to plan for a future that is simply uncertain. The only thing that's truly stable is the reality that instability abounds.

BECOMING A STRANGER

A third challenging aspect to being a stranger in a strange land is the experience of falling out of step with what's viewed as a normal life within your community.

I once took a class at an urban, multiethnic seminary attended by students from all walks of life. One day a Black student from one of the United States' most violent cities shared how her adult son had been killed in a drive-by shooting just a few weeks prior. The difference in reaction among the suburban white and inner-city Black students was remarkable. I and the other white suburbanites were dumbfounded. We knew such things happened, but I didn't know anyone who had experienced this particular form of tragedy and suffering. The Black students who lived in much more dangerous environments had a very different response, captured well in the words of one: "Oh no, honey, you too?"

Notice how my fellow student's experience isolated her from the experience of her white classmates.[1] If we were to understand her, she had to explain her experience to us. At the same time, her suffering connected her to her own community, where so many others had experienced similar suffering. Here she did not need to explain the torrent of emotions, questions, and struggles she now faced. The people around her already understood on a deeply visceral level.

A significant challenge of being a chronic pain and illness family is that your struggles are not shared by many within your community. You muster up the energy and willingness to attend a church small group and share some of your story, only to be told, "I'm so sorry to hear that. We will love to have you join us for activities whenever you feel well enough to come." The person who utters these words isn't intending to be cruel. But right there you've been isolated as *different*. The community has a normal pattern of how life is lived, and you fall outside it. Come and join if you can, but if you can't, know we'll miss you.

Church can often seem like the pounding surf of insurmountable tasks: join small groups, volunteer for children's ministry, go to the men's or women's retreat, be part of this evangelistic event. Serve! Serve! Serve! All of these are good things and part of the normal spiritual patterns of many families, but when you're eating your third frozen pizza of the week for dinner and it's only Tuesday, these expectations of what good church members do feel overwhelmingly out of reach. It's not your beliefs that set you apart; it's that your life pattern is an entirely different shape—the jagged shape of surviving—one that can't smoothly follow the "normal" lines of prescribed church involvement.

We see the same isolationism happen when browsing through the plethora of Christian living books promising how to have a happy, functioning, God-centered family. Have nightly family worship! Date your wife! Schedule intentional getaways with your children for focused discipleship and spirituality building!

Such things sound wonderful, don't they? But over here in the world of chronic pain and illness, it's Wednesday, and I'm doing pretty well to have clean clothes for people to wear for school tomorrow.

Being unable to live up to the pattern of what some say is necessary for healthy spirituality can sometimes give rise to anxiety, fear, and guilt. *What if I'm crippling my children's chances to follow Jesus by not doing intentional Bible studies with them? What if my marriage is headed toward the rocks because we can't go on date nights?* So often these helpful and valid *suggestions* for how to live out the Bible's teaching can overreach into becoming *necessary*. Dating your wife becomes *the* way that you fireproof your marriage. Not being able to sustain a family devotional time with any regularity ratchets up worries that one day your children will tread the path of the Prodigal Son—without the coming-home part.

It's important to remember that despite whatever certain books or speakers may claim, none of these specifics are essential to having a godly family. They're all time-and-culture-bound expressions of how to live out the teachings of the Bible. "Love your wife" is a timeless biblical truth for all husbands at all times. "Date your wife" is one way to apply this, but it assumes that you have the health, flexibility, community, and financial ability to do so. You aren't sinning by not being able to sustain these suggested ways of applying biblical truths. You're not even being unwise. The truth is that your circumstances are strange, and being a stranger in a strange land means that your patterns and practices will likely look different from others around you.

The early church consisted largely of day laborers who received a small silver coin (a denarius) at the end of each workday that enabled them to buy enough food to get them through to the next day. If they could make it to the end and hear "Well done, good and faithful servant" from their Lord, then surely we can as well. Raising your kids in the fear and admonition of the Lord may look like having a conversation about who made the trees on the way to school. The Lord is pleased with you when you do what you can with the time that you have. And after that, we leave the rest in his kind hands.

SO WHAT DO YOU DO ABOUT IT?

This whole chapter has been marching toward a terribly difficult question. For all the living as a stranger in a strange land, the isolation, the instability, the feeling like an outsider—what do you then do about it?

The first step is traveling some of the roads you and I have already traveled together in the first two chapters of this book. Christianity is a dose of realism in a world that so often desperately tries to deny reality. Philosopher Thomas Hobbes famously wrote that life in the state of nature is "solitary, poor, nasty, brutish, short."[2] And while God's grace may hold us back from experiencing all these depressing adjectives to their fullest extent, Hobbes and the author of Ecclesiastes would certainly find some common ground.

As hard as it is, we all have to let go of the dreams that we once had. Life isn't Plan A anymore, and many things you wish would be simply will not. Pastor John Piper offers you and me words that are ruggedly real: "Occasionally, weep deeply over the life that you hoped would be. Grieve the losses. Feel the pain. Then wash your face, trust God, and embrace the life that he's given you."[3]

The life of a chronic pain and illness family can be terribly clarifying, like the first rays of sun after a torrential thunderstorm.

The chaos and instability of life can serve to reduce the actual elements of following the Lord down to their simplest forms.

Be kind to one another.
Ask forgiveness when you aren't.
Weep together.
Endure hardship.
Work hard.
Worship God.
Rest.
Be patient with those who don't get it.
Use your energy to serve your kids and your spouse.
Find a small way to care for one person outside your family who also hurts.

It's easy to worry if you're doing these things right or enough. But at the end of the day the list of things that are required for us to look like Christ is far simpler than most of us imagine. What would pursuing faithful simplicity look like for you right now? If you're able, make a list of things that need to be modified for the sake of survival and long-term endurance and talk about them with your loved one. Stripping life back to these basic elements isn't a panacea against sadness. Faithfulness doesn't make the sorrow and pain of life go away. But it does give us a trustworthy path to follow as we live as aliens and strangers in the land of our own lives.

4

GOD, INTERRUPTED

While I was growing up, my family had a tradition of watching a movie every Friday night. Over the years we transitioned from a broad array of kids' cartoons to dramas and action movies. One Friday late into high school, we sat down to watch an epic naval drama set during the golden age of sail. We had been looking forward to this movie for weeks. What we didn't realize was that we were about to walk straight into a scene in which a doctor performs surgery on himself without anesthetics to remove a bullet from his abdomen.

My family of origin was good at many things, but enduring graphic depictions of medical procedures was not one of them. The family room emptied one by one, leaving the television blaring on as each of us manufactured excuses to escape the images on the screen. Popcorn was popped, bathroom breaks were taken, and I'm pretty sure I cleaned my room, which was a rare event for me as a high schooler.

Think what you may of my family of origin's squeamishness toward simulated surgery, but most of us struggle to sit and look with an unblinking eye at suffering. Our culture struggles to face pervasive, life-dominating pain without breaking eye contact. We tend to rush our relationship to suffering due to natural discomfort with loss and ruination. Struggling to behold suffering often leads to flat advice about how to endure such circumstances. "Suffer well," we say, as though someone whose life has been upended needs to hear us tell them not to let their suffering go to waste.

A friend of mine and fellow counselor puts our tendency to ignore the very real human struggle in suffering this way:

> If you've heard the phrase "suffer well"... once, then you've likely heard it a few 100 times. When I hear it, here's what I hear:
>
> "Suffer well. Buck up! God works all things together for good. Quit the pity party. Don't you know you can and should hope in God!? Deny your feelings. Faith matters, not feelings. Grow up. Stop complaining. Be happy. Count your blessings."
>
> I fear that "suffer well" has become an evangelical code ... for "stop feeling!"[1]

Sometimes characters from the Bible can be used to support a vision of suffering that expects people to take hits and just keep moving. The apostle Paul's rugged missionary life is one of these stories. He mentions his struggles in various places throughout his letters, yet he consistently and quickly moves on to how God strengthens him. Writing to his friends in Corinth, he tells them,

> We don't want you to be unaware, brothers and sisters, of our affliction that took place in Asia. We were completely overwhelmed—beyond our strength—so that we even despaired of life itself. Indeed, we felt that we had received the sentence of death, so that we would not trust in ourselves but in God

who raises the dead. He has delivered us from such a terrible death, and he will deliver us. We have put our hope in him that he will deliver us again. (2 Cor. 1:8–10)

Elsewhere we find Paul writing from house arrest, "Rejoice in the Lord always. I will say it again: Rejoice!" (Phil. 4:4). After being attacked by a crowd, beaten with rods by the local police force, and thrown into prison, Paul and his traveling companion Silas are pictured as praying and singing hymns around midnight (Acts 16:25).

Suffering never seems to get Paul down. And if it does, this missionary dynamo is always ready with a quick theological meditation on God's goodness and strength before he gets back to work. He has zero moments of questioning God, no internal monologue of disillusionment or confusion.

PAUL, YOU MAKE ME FEEL TIRED

I don't know about you, but when I read all these words from Paul, my first response is usually to feel very tired. And my second response is a creeping feeling of shame that I'm not handling suffering the "biblical way" like Paul. I seem to have a lot more trouble processing things than he did.

But before we despair over how our spiritual experience is substandard compared to Paul's, we have to remember something about Paul's description of his sufferings. Paul tends to write his conclusions, his heart's view after he's finished climbing and reached the top. We don't know much of Paul's internal dialogue about the sweat and the burn on the climb up because he didn't write about that. He emphasizes God's work and our outcome, not his own internal process of struggle. We don't know what those dark nights were like before Paul started singing, or what the voice in his head was saying as he despaired of life itself.

There is a thread running through the Bible about how we triumph over suffering. This topic is so important, because our experience of chronic pain and illness would be truly terrible if there were no promise that Jesus conquered death and is preparing a place for us where there is no more crying, pain, and death. We'll return to this triumph in chapter 8.

But alongside that promise of triumph is a dark current of deep trouble written into the Bible. Although we may not be as familiar with these people or these stories, the Bible does not shy away from deep, dark spiritual struggles due to intense suffering. God does not just give us Paul's conclusions; he also gives us other authors who speak of their own journeys through the labyrinth of their own crises of faith due to suffering.

ASAPH: THE SONGWRITER WHO ALMOST WALKED AWAY FROM GOD

Asaph isn't a household name in our day and age, but he would have been in ancient Israel. Twelve of his hymns are included in the Bible as psalms, including hits like Psalm 81:

> Sing for joy to God our strength;
> shout in triumph to the God of Jacob.
> Lift up a song—play the tambourine,
> the melodious lyre, and the harp. (vv. 1–2)

Elsewhere he exults in God's goodness, power, and mercy, recalling how Yahweh had "shepherded [Israel] with a pure heart and guided them with his skillful hands" (Ps. 78:72).

Yet Asaph's brilliant joy in Yahweh is not all he writes about. Asaph's psalms contain the meditations of a man deeply troubled with sorrow. In Psalm 73, he writes, "As for me, my feet almost slipped; my steps nearly went astray" (v. 2). We don't know the specifics, but Asaph metaphorically stood on the edge of a harrowing precipice. His path narrowed, becoming just wide enough for a pair of feet to cross this harrowing strand of trail. To his left stood a sheer cliff, nothing to hold on to. To his right, a yawning precipice opened onto the jagged rocks below. To slip was to plunge to his death.

Asaph does not edge away from just how close he was to losing his footing as he traveled the path of deep sorrow. There was the sudden slide of feet out from under him, the windmilling of the arms, the flash of panic as adrenaline coursed through his body. It was a coin flip as to whether he would lose his faith or not.

What caused this songwriter such trouble? First, he suffered: "I am afflicted all day long and punished every morning" (Ps. 73:14). And second, he saw that those less righteous than he did not suffer the same way: "I saw the prosperity of the wicked. They have an easy time until they die.... They are not in trouble like others.... They are always at ease" (Ps. 73:3–4, 5, 12).

For Asaph, this question led him to struggle in his relationship with God. He writes,

> I think of God; I groan;
> I meditate; my spirit becomes weak. (Ps. 77:3)

> Will the Lord reject forever
> and never again show favor?
> Has his faithful love ceased forever? (vv. 7–8)

> Has God forgotten to be gracious?
> Has he in anger withheld his compassion? (v. 9)

Asaph's soul cries out in anguish as Scripture itself provides no comfort for his spirit and turning to God produces groaning: "I am grieved that the right hand of the Most High has changed" (Ps. 77:10). In the depth of his suffering, Asaph's tentative conclusion is that God is different than he was before. God's faithfulness has ceased; he has become a mystery.

For all of Asaph's theological knowledge and prior personal experience with God, he could not make sense of his suffering. "When I tried to understand all this, it seemed hopeless" (Ps. 73:16). The sheer irrationality of suffering drove him to the brink of declaring that God was not God and that all was meaningless.

Each year Kate and I have to commemorate multiple unwanted anniversaries: the date of the surgery that changed life forever, the date of an accident that plunged her deeper into unexplained pain. They are days of darkness and sorrow, and ones we dread. "Rejoice always" seems like a cruel taunt on those days. We connect far better with Asaph's exhausted, messy weakness on those days than with Paul's triumphant conclusions.

Of course, our turmoil is not confined to just two days on the calendar. Anxiety spikes as a new symptom emerges. *Is this a normal ache and pain that will pass, or is it another slip down from the plateau we've been on to a decreased new normal?* Hopelessness swells as day after day of intense pain slows life to a crawl. If you're anything like me, far too often it sure feels like you're fighting the bad fight, dropping out of the race, and not quite guaranteed to keep the faith.

JOB: THE MOST RIGHTEOUS PERSON ON EARTH

Paul tells us little of his internal meditations, while Asaph provides only a few of the specific circumstances surrounding his troubles. In Job, we get both the story and his dark and troubled processing of it. And the details are disturbing.

Job is singled out for suffering because he is the most upright person on earth. God himself says of Job, "No one else on earth is like him, a man of perfect integrity, who fears God and turns away from evil" (Job 1:8). Thus every horror unleashed in Job's life is not because he's bad but specifically because he is so righteous. The second most righteous person on earth does not earn Job's suffering; Job does.

Satan, the accuser whose lies served as the catalyst for the ruination of the human race and the created world, appears before God. And this evil being, the one who was cast from heaven because he tried to usurp God's own throne, has a plan for God's finest son. He wants to put God's worthiness of worship to the test by raining down destruction on Job: "Stretch out your hand and strike everything he owns, and he will surely curse you to your face" (Job 1:11).

And God says yes.

All of Job's great wealth is swallowed up by raiding parties and natural disasters. But that's only Satan's first act. A ragged servant runs up to Job and utters the worst news of all: "Your sons and daughters were eating and drinking wine in their oldest brother's house. Suddenly a powerful wind swept in from the desert and struck the four corners of the house. It collapsed on the young people so that they died" (Job 1:18–19).

I don't know about you, but I find this account deeply troubling. Job's children are all gone in an instant. Seven sons. Three daughters. Ten corpses retrieved from under the rubble of a cratered house. And all because God said yes to Satan's request to unravel Job's life.

Job's immediate response is remarkable. He tears his robe and shaves his head—a sign of deep mourning in his ancient culture. He falls to the ground and worships, uttering the kind of words that we later will see from the apostle Paul—theologically rich and courageous—bearing up well under great loss: "Naked I came from my mother's womb, and naked I will leave this life. The LORD gives, and the LORD takes away. Blessed be the name of the LORD" (Job 1:21).

But that's not the end of Job's misery. Having failed to destroy Job, Satan returns to God and asks to further shatter this man's world. God gives Job the wages of more suffering as recompense for his faithful response to the first round of trouble. God looks at Satan and says of Job, "He is in your power" (Job 2:6). Bereft of all his comforts in life, deeply grieving the loss of the children he cherished, Job's body rebels and "terrible boils" bubble up "from the soles of his feet to the top of his head" (v. 7). No matter how Job arranges his body, he finds no relief, only renewed agony. When his friends arrive, they find righteous Job so ruined and ragged that "when they looked from a distance, they could barely recognize him. They wept aloud" (v. 12).

His wealth is gone, his children are dead, and his body is so mangled that his friends no longer recognize him. All because God says yes to Satan's request to destroy Job.

JOB AFTER WE TEND TO STOP READING

If you've heard the story of Job told many times, you'll notice something peculiar about the way we handle his account. We read Job 1–2, then skip to the end where God starts speaking to Job from the whirlwind. After some forthright words from the Lord to Job, the book wraps up with God restoring Job in the happy ending.

I get it! The middle section of Job is a lengthy conversation that is often a confusing tumble of words. But throughout these speeches, Job weaves together his own internal troubles and trembles at what has befallen him. And there we find a man who is devastated by his pain and wrestling with his sense of who God is. Read his words here slowly, taking in the fullness of what he's trying to communicate:

> May the day I was born perish,
> and the night that said,
> "A boy is conceived." (Job 3:3)

> Why was I not stillborn;
> why didn't I die as I came from the womb?
> . . . Then I would be at rest. (vv. 11, 13)

> Why is light given to one burdened with grief,
> and life to those whose existence is bitter,
> who wait for death, but it does not come,
> and search for it more than for hidden treasure,
> who are filled with much joy
> and are glad when they reach the grave? (vv. 20–22)

For the thing I feared has overtaken me,
and what I dreaded has happened to me.
I cannot relax or be calm;
I have no rest, for turmoil has come. (vv. 25–26)

Job would rather be dead than live the life he's currently living, wracked with pain and bereft of his children and comforts. These aren't the good Christian niceties that we often expect godly men and women to say. Imagine standing up in your church or small group and saying, "I wish I had never been born, and I do not understand why God won't just let me die." Yet here we have the godliest man alive starting his very first speech that way.

Job wasn't unclear about who ultimately held the keys to his suffering. He does not rail against the universe for its random cruelty or curse his luck. He lays the responsibility for his suffering at the feet of God himself:

Surely the arrows of the Almighty have pierced me;
my spirit drinks their poison.
God's terrors are arrayed against me. (Job 6:4)

He batters me with a whirlwind
and multiplies my wounds without cause.
He doesn't let me catch my breath
but fills me with bitter experiences. (9:17–18)

Your hands shaped me and formed me.
Will you now turn and destroy me?
Please remember that you formed me like clay.
Will you now return me to dust? (10:8–9)

Job does not shy away from rooting the suffering he is experiencing in God's will. Satan may be the proximate cause for his suffering, the catalyst for his ruination. But Job knows that whatever befalls him can happen only if God permits it. Each of the ten limp bodies of his children that he buried, every oozing boil and flash of unrelenting pain, has as its ultimate fountainhead the sovereign allowance of God.

And friend, our story is no different from Job's. Saying God has nothing to do with our suffering may seem a convenient way of preserving his goodness; however, the truth is that Job is right. God is the one who says of himself, "I declare the end from the beginning, and from long ago what is not yet done, saying: my plan will take place, and I will do all my will" (Isa. 46:10). Nothing happens apart from his permission.

Does this trouble you? It does me. Sovereignty feels more comfortable when times are good. But it's a hard hurdle when you watch your spouse or child or parent or grandchild be taken apart piece by piece. God and I have had many conversations about why he led us on a path to a doctor whose advice destroyed my wife's life and sucked our whole family down with it. I struggle to understand how God has the audacity to give us a book that reads, "The LORD is good and upright" (Ps. 25:8) while also telling Satan yes when he asks permission to kill Job's ten children. What kind of God dares to describe himself as "compassionate and gracious . . . slow to anger and abounding in faithful love and truth" (Ex. 34:6) and then chooses to steer our paths to suffering and withholds healing when he could give it in an instant? What kind of God buffets us with one tragedy after another when life is already hard enough as it is?

Suddenly there's a fresh complexity to singing songs both old and new. Kate and I chose an old hymn extolling God's goodness as our wedding hymn:

> Great is thy faithfulness, Lord God Almighty;
> There is no shadow of turning with thee;
> Thou changest not; thy compassions, they fail not;
> As thou hast been, thou forever wilt be.[2]

That song evokes far more questions and puzzlement now than it did when we stood opposite each other and took our vows. I still affirm the truths captured in this beautiful song, but what is meant by God's compassions failing not is far more puzzling than when we sang about them on an aggressively hot day in the California sun.

Job knew what this kind of mixed-up relationship with God was like. He struggled to put together God's unchanging goodness and God's actions toward him. At times he looked at God and perceived him as a punisher, an adversary.

> Are my days not few? Stop it!
> Leave me alone, so that I can smile a little
> before I go to a land of darkness and gloom,
> never to return. (Job 10:20–21)

Do these words seem ungodly to you? Remember, it was a godly person of the Bible who spoke them. Job is only mentioned once in the Scriptures outside the book that bears his name. Jesus's half brother James calls Christians to remember "the steadfastness of Job" (James 5:11 ESV). This does not mean that Job was sinless or that every word that passed across his lips was wise. But it does mean that Job's faithfulness was manifest through his questions, troubles, and groans. God looks at Job's anguish-driven doubts and says "steadfast," not "unfaithful."

Our culture doesn't tend to feel particularly comfortable in conversations about suffering that don't wrap up with a tidy comment about God's enduring faithfulness. I often struggle knowing how to end conversations with friends who inquire about how we are doing, especially when the honest answer is "not well." There's a pressure to tie sufferings up with a nice bow, to whitewash sorrow and pain with a cheerful coat of paint. Ending a conversation at the point of lament leaves me feeling like a killjoy or someone who isn't full of gospel hope.

Do you ever feel this way? Does it seem like your sorrow and suffering are unwelcome or that you cannot truly speak of what's going on in your heart? If that is the case, friend, know that God does not shy away from your pain. He is not uncomfortable with your questions or dismayed by your tears. What we've seen in this chapter is not the only thing to be said about suffering. The next chapter will turn more to the hope and help that God gives. But for now, we can leave things alongside Job and Asaph and others. Having deep questions about God is not a sign of unfaithfulness. There's a long line of godly men and women in the Bible who did not understand God's actions and did not pretend to do so. We must sometimes patiently wade through uncomfortable and disquieting questions dredged up during intense storms previously unexperienced in our lives. Those questions and struggles do not make you ungodly.

5

WE ARE DUST

STEP INTO THE WORLD of ultramarathoning for a moment and you'll quickly find top athletes raving about an often overlooked member of their team: the pacer. Many ultramarathons last more than twenty-four hours, and sending a deeply fatigued runner, no matter how experienced, out into the dark to climb hills alone in remote areas is usually a bad idea. The pacer runs alongside the athlete and helps them endure through the toughest moments. The pacer is an encouragement when you feel like giving up. They're a touchpoint with reality if hallucinations develop. They're an emergency medic should something go terribly awry.

The pacer highlights human weakness and is a physical representation of our need. Even the most seasoned and finely trained runners in the world often don't go it alone—for the sake of both their success and safety. Think of how God describes the ones he has crafted in his image: "He knows what we are made of, remembering that we are dust" (Ps. 103:14). Like exhausted runners staggering on toward a still-distant finish line, you and I are frail, both physically and spiritually.

One of the songs that's been part of my church experience for the last thirty years similarly underscores my weakness and frailty:

> Prone to wander, Lord, I feel it.
> Prone to leave the God I love.[1]

Ironically, I've seen the first of these two lines emblazoned on home décor, phone cases, and Christmas ornaments. But this phrase doesn't speak of a desire to burst outside and lose oneself on a solitary hiking trail. The next line makes clear that we're singing of our tendency to lose the path. At times you and I will need to have our hearts drawn back toward God and his truth. Such is the case for every redeemed human being, for we are a collection of people who are prone to both great triumphs of faith and surprising moments of great failure.

Wouldn't it be wonderful if the pain and pressure of wading through the waters of chronic pain and illness left us immune to attack? Life's hard enough without having to keep a keen eye out for the roaring lion that would seek to devour us. Vigilance seems a cruel ask for the weary, and yet the reality is that deep suffering often provides fertile ground for trouble. If idle hands are the devil's workshop, then pain would seem to be his storage shed. Sadness easily metastasizes into bitterness. Frustration begets unwarranted anger. Helplessness morphs into despair.

Given this reality, how can we tell if we're veering off the path or not? The very real questions about God discussed in the last chapter are scary. How can we know if they're the product of a heart that loves the Lord or one that's hardening toward him? God warns us to "take care, brothers and sisters, that there will not be in any one of you an evil, unbelieving heart that falls away from the living God" (Heb. 3:12 NASB). How can we tell if our hearts are rebelling or crying out in pain from deep wounds?

Thankfully, the same God who invites us to express our pain also helps us discern whether our hearts are plodding along in faithfulness or stumbling through the off-path underbrush. Let's revisit our friends Job and Asaph from the last chapter to see what they discover. Along the way we'll also meet other friends who bear the scars of deep spiritual struggle.

FAITHFUL QUESTIONING AND UNFAITHFUL QUESTIONING

Almost a third of the Psalms' 150 chapters are devoted to some kind of lament. Most of these songs sourced from pain and trouble follow a pattern of describing difficulty and then ending with a reaffirmation of God's enduring faithfulness and loyal love. But some of them do not. Consider these two verses, the first written by David and the second by Heman:

> Turn Your eyes away from me, that I may become cheerful again
> Before I depart and am no more. (Ps. 39:13 NASB)

> You have distanced loved one and neighbor from me; darkness is my only friend. (Ps. 88:18)

Both verses close out their respective psalms, and both are stark complaints against God himself. *Leave me alone. You've made it so that darkness is my friend, not you.* Such language seems to dance along the border of unfaithfulness, doesn't it? After all, it is in God's presence that there is fullness of joy (Ps. 16:11); he is light, and in him is no darkness (1 John 1:5).

These words sound like they're in the same key as other far less faithful statements:

> [The wicked one] says to himself, "God has forgotten; he hides his face and will never see." (Ps. 10:11)

> The fool says in his heart, "There's no God." (Ps. 14:1)

Here we come to a critical fork in the road in our discussion about having a complicated relationship with God. There is a way to question and wonder that is faithful, and there's a way to do it that is unfaithful. Jesus says that the way is narrow, and we want to make sure that we travel the narrow way that leads to life and not the broad way that leads to death.

Author and pastor Tim Keller significantly helped me understand why the cries of these two psalmists and others like them are faithful and not ungodly declarations.[2] These words are prayers, spoken in the context of a relationship of love and commitment. Heman begins his complaint by addressing it to the "Lord, God of my salvation" (Ps. 88:1). David likewise begs God to "hear my prayer, Lord, and listen to my cry for help" (Ps. 39:12). Their cries of feeling abandoned are voiced to God and still express a faith, however faint, that God is their hope.

There are two kinds of hearts that say bitter things. One says bitter things out of bitter rejection of God. The other says bitter things out of deep pain, yet the words are drawn from bewilderment and not rebellion. Theologian Tremper Longman III remarks in his commentary on Psalm 88 that it is "one of the bleakest of all the prayers in the book, but still it is a prayer, and, unlike the grumblers in the wilderness, the psalmist continues to turn to God to voice his anguish and call for aid."[3]

Our friends from the last chapter lived this reality as well. Job's terror of God stems from every indication that God's nearness will crush him further. And yet at the same time, Job does not stray from a deep commitment to that God. Even in the midst of his pain, he cries out,

Even if he kills me, I will hope in him. (Job 13:15)

But I know that my Redeemer lives,
and at the end he will stand on the dust.
Even after my skin has been destroyed,
yet I will see God in my flesh.
I will see him myself;
my eyes will look at him, and not as a stranger.
My heart longs within me. (Job 19:25–27)

God is not a stranger to Job but a friend whom he longs to be with. Asaph too spoke of God as his friend and strength, even amid his trouble:

Who do I have in heaven but you?
And I desire nothing on earth but you.
My flesh and my heart may fail,
but God is the strength of my heart,
my portion forever. (Ps. 73:25–26)

There is a tremendous gap between how a righteous and an unrighteous heart respond to God. The righteous heart says, "I may not understand you, and I may be deeply puzzled at the road you've allowed me to walk, but I will not walk away from you." The unrighteous heart does not share this humility but shakes its fist at the heavens and refuses to submit to a God it fails to comprehend.

What Kate and I have walked through has caused crises of faith for both of us. We've asked questions of God that we never thought we would ask. We've been forced to adjudicate anew our beliefs about his existence, his goodness, his power. Your journey may have driven you to ask such questions as well. Whatever your path looks like, you ultimately are on a collision course with a stark reality: God is different from us, and we do not fully understand him.

> "For my thoughts are not your thoughts,
> and your ways are not my ways."
> This is the LORD's declaration.
> "For as heaven is higher than earth,
> so my ways are higher than your ways,
> and my thoughts than your thoughts." (Isa. 55:8–9)

God never calls us to fully understand him. He calls us to love him, to trust him, and to obey him. At the end of the day, when all the chips are down, this is the question. It's the same question that Satan posed to God all those years ago: "Does Job fear God for nothing? Haven't you placed a hedge around him, his household, and everything he owns? . . . But stretch out your hand and strike everything he owns, and he will surely curse you to your face" (Job 1:9–11).

We are like Peter, sifted like wheat (Luke 22:31). We are like Sarah, mystified by God's seemingly unanswered promises

(Gen. 18:12). We are like Habakkuk, perplexed at God's lack of rescue (Hab. 1:2). We are like Naomi, emptied by loss (Ruth 1:20–21). We are like John the Baptist, growing in questions as the cost piles up (Matt. 11:3).

And yet, all of these answered their own questions with faith. They did not always understand God, his ways, or his works, but that is not the call for us as Christians. The call is to trust the God who is beyond us, allowing questions and faith to stand side by side.

FRIEND, YOU'RE GOING TO SIN

There is one more lesson we need to take from our friends Job and Asaph before we move on from their stories. As much as we may wish to talk only about suffering, we also have to talk about sin. Because, friend, there is no beating around the bush—I have sinned in my walk alongside my wife, and you will sin in your walk alongside your loved one. Listen for a moment to our friend Asaph as he reflects upon his journey into darkness:

> When I became embittered
> and my innermost being was wounded,
> I was stupid and didn't understand;
> I was an unthinking animal toward you. (Ps. 73:21–22)

Asaph doesn't hide the fact that he veered off the path. His heart moved from questioning to bitterness under the influence of his pain, and his mind pitched over the cliff of being perplexed into believing untruth. Asaph does not flee from describing himself as sinning.

Job did not survive his ordeal unscathed either. After he proclaimed that he would prove to God how unjustly he was being treated, God indeed showed up. God's very first words make it clear that Job will not emerge victorious in this encounter:

> Who is this who obscures my counsel
> with ignorant words?
> Get ready to answer me like a man;
> when I question you, you will inform me. (Job 38:2–3)

God compares Job's resume to his own across the next three chapters, after which all Job can do is recant:

> Surely I spoke about things I did not understand,
> things too wondrous for me to know. (Job 42:3)

> Therefore, I reject my words and am sorry for them;
> I am dust and ashes. (v. 6)

These two men are godly, faithful examples of bearing up well under soul-bending suffering. And at the same time, they were also human beings whose hearts cracked under the crushing weight of their oppressive circumstances.

You and I are not better than Job and Asaph. There are times when I close my eyes at night proud of how I have handled the day's challenges. And there are plenty of other days when I say with David, "I know my wrongdoings, and my sin is constantly before me" (Ps. 51:3 NASB).

We need to talk about sin because it is a reality. None of us are righteous through and through. Sin is corrosive to relationships. It's destructive to our souls. It shunts us off the path of flourishing onto a path that wanders through arid wasteland. Our ability to bear up under the heavy load of loving someone afflicted with chronic pain and illness is directly related to our ability to discern when we're beginning to leave the path and plant the seeds of deep trouble in our lives and relationships.

Over the last several years, I've had significant bouts with anger, impatience, despair, callousness, peevishness, envy, and a long list of other troubles. There's always a voice in my heart whispering, "You wouldn't be struggling with this if it wasn't for these circumstances. Your wrongdoing is not really your fault."

It's true that being hard-pressed by my wife's health troubles has brought my weakness into stark relief; however, no amount of pain, sleeplessness, and solo parenting created them. Jesus looks at me and says, "A good person produces good out of the good stored up in his heart. An evil person produces evil out of the evil stored up in his heart, for his mouth speaks from the overflow of the heart" (Luke 6:45). As a follower of Christ, I am redeemed and renewed, sealed with the Holy Spirit. However, all Christians still struggle with plenty of indwelling sin that's slowly being purged out of their hearts. Every harsh and hasty word, every unpleasant attitude, every time I succumb to temptation rather than mastering it comes from those still-sinful impulses that reside within me. I am always at fault for my own sin. I can't blame Kate's struggles, the crumpled heap of our family life, the narrow budget, or any other challenge that I face. And as it is for me, so it is for you. No matter how different your spouse is, no matter how great the grief over your child's struggles, no matter how hard-pressed things become, your unrighteousness always comes from within you.

And friend, that is why we need Jesus. If there's one shining beacon of truth in the midst of your journey as a person who loves another beset by chronic pain and illness, it's that you cannot do this on your own. You need Christ desperately, just the same as I do. We need his strength to hold up our drooping hands. We need the hope that he bought for us by his resurrection. We need his cleansing, which he offers to us without payment or price.

The beautiful words of 1 John 1:8–9 are written to you right now:

> If we say, "We have no sin," we are deceiving ourselves, and the truth is not in us. If we confess our sins, he is faithful and righteous to forgive us our sins and to cleanse us from all unrighteousness.

As with Job and Asaph, God does not meet us in our sins to terrify us. He is the God who is full of mercy, delighting in repentance. God is not a glowering Father who finds wild-eyed joy in beating the unrighteousness out of us. He draws us to repentance in kindness and meets us with the joy of a Father whose long-lost child has returned home.

If these last few paragraphs are like another language to you, I'd encourage you to turn to the back of this book and read appendix A. There you'll find more on what it means to submit your heart to God and be reconciled to him. And if you find yourself ashamed of your sins, look up to Christ. He delights in casting the penalty of your sins as far from you as the east is from the west.

HELP NAVIGATING THE MAZE

As I mentioned in this book's introduction, I'm a counseling professor. I spend most of my time teaching students how to help others navigate life mazes, sort through thoughts and emotions, evaluate choices, uncover subconscious lenses that color the way they view the world, and work through relational challenges.

One thing I quickly discovered on our chronic pain and illness journey is that teaching others how to navigate life's mazes and navigating my own are two different adventures. The view from the sky and the view from the ground—where every wall looks the same and every path seems to lead to yet another dead end—are significantly different.

Having a heart that's prone to wander means that I need help from others to keep me on right paths. Quoleth wrote in his wisdom that "two are better than one . . . for if either falls, his companion can lift him up; but pity the one who falls without another to lift him up" (Eccl. 4:9–10). God has blessed me with a small cohort of friends who are willing to see and know me, who are unafraid of hard questions and tearful conversations. Take a moment and ask yourself,

- Who can you talk to when your envy of other "normal" families wells up?
- Who can you talk to when you feel alienated from your church community or abandoned by those around you who you thought would care?
- Who can you talk to when your baseline worries and anxieties break through your natural defenses and grind you to a halt or spin you up into anger?
- Who can you talk to when you deeply desire sex but your spouse is sexually unavailable?
- Who can you talk to about your deepest questions about God and his character?

There may not be one person who is able to walk with you through every category of trouble and challenge you face. Wisdom is required when you think about who is safe and helpful.

I've long considered the image of a medical research facility as a helpful metaphor for wisely sharing my heart with others. Imagine stepping into that secure facility. You enter through the rotating doors and are met by a receptionist. Everyone is allowed inside the lobby and met with a friendly greeting, but to go any farther you need a lab-issued electronic keycard. Certain visitors may be able to tour a handful of rooms, and junior researchers may be allowed to go still farther. But the deepest rooms in the building are accessible only by a few senior personnel whose experience qualifies them to handle sensitive equipment and specimens in such a way as to avoid catastrophe.

Everyone is able to access the lobby of our family's life. Kate and I both freely talk about the fact that chronic pain and illness is part of our story. Someone needs to know about us in order to know us, and the effects of Kate's chronic pain and illness are some of the defining elements of who we are.

While everyone's allowed in the lobby, the rooms beyond it are more carefully guarded. Even in this book I've been careful not to bring into focus the specifics of what exactly has gone wrong with Kate's physiology. Some people know, but it's not for public consumption.

There are others in our life who are not privy to the inner workings of our hearts. When I'm asked, "How are you doing?" there are plenty of times that I'll say, "Doing good," even when in those moments I'm really imploding. Why? Because that person has lobby clearance, not epidemiology lab clearance.

The apostle John portrays Jesus practicing wise gatekeeping with the crowds, as he "would not entrust himself to them, since he knew them all" (John 2:24). While we may long for relationships and churches where everyone is safe and responds helpfully, the reality is that our communities are a mix of different spiritual and personal maturities. Wisdom recognizes that a higher security clearance is dependent upon deeper, more trusting relationships.

In my life, there is no one person who knows absolutely everything about me. But everything is known by someone, even those things that I'd prefer in my pride to keep hidden from others. When a medical team performs surgery, no one person does every medically necessary task. The surgeon, anesthesiologist, and sanitation team have different roles, all of which are essential for successful surgery. It's a team effort, and it takes the whole team to care well for the patient who stands needing significant help. My friend, let me encourage you to be known by your spouse. Be known by friends. Be known by those who are faithful spiritual guides. We may be prone to wander, but God has not left us alone to figure out only by painful experience when we're starting to veer from the well-trodden paths of righteousness.

6

RENEGOTIATING RELATIONSHIPS

I think Justin O. Schmidt is crazy, and I'm willing to wager you might too. Schmidt is an entomologist who has dedicated his life to creating a scale to rank the pain produced by various insect bites and stings. The only way to do this is to actually be bitten or stung, so he has offered himself up to 150 different species of pain-producing bugs, all in the name of science.

Toward the low end of the scale sits the red fire ant, rated a pain level 1. Schmidt writes of this common species, "Sharp, sudden, mildly alarming. Like walking across a shag carpet and reaching for the light switch." Move higher on the chart and the descriptions become far more intense. The warrior wasp captures a coveted position as a level 4 insect (the top level). Schmidt waxes eloquent: "Torture. You are chained in the flow of an active volcano." Another level 4, the bullet ant, brings "pure, intense, brilliant pain. Like walking over flaming charcoal with a 3-inch nail embedded in your heel."[1]

I, for one, am glad that God has set me on a very different vocational path from Justin O. Schmidt. Yet his career highlights something fascinating about pain. One wouldn't think that an insect measuring less than two inches in length could create such agony. Look at a grizzly bear, and it's clear from the outset that something that large with enormous teeth and claws can do some serious damage. But pound for pound, the bullet ant certainly punches above its weight class.

Relational pain is a nearer neighbor to the bullet ant than the grizzly bear. It hurts far more than you'd think. It's not difficult to see why a broken arm hurts so much when you look at an X-ray and see the damage that's been done. But relational pain is more mysterious, less tangible. Why does it sting so much when people do things that hurt your spirit?

God designed us in his image as intensely relational beings, desiring us to interact both with himself and with other humans. Adam's relationship with God began the first moment clay turned into living flesh. And the absence of another human for Adam to relate to spurred God to pronounce the words "not good" over his almost-finished creation. As we saw in chapter 2, God does not tell us much about Eden or how our ancestors were driven from it, but he highlights relational joy and relational breakdown throughout the story of creation and the fall. Relational pain hurts so badly because it's a direct strike against one of the most important things that makes us human.

In this chapter, we will look at how your relationships with other people get swept up in the tidal wave of chronic pain and illness. We'll first turn to your relationship with your loved one, then discuss your relationship with those outside your family unit.

YOUR RELATIONSHIP WITH YOUR LOVED ONE

All of us have moments in life that get seared into our memories. One of mine is opening up my computer one day and reading words my wife published about her journey: "The old Kate is gone. I don't think I will ever see her again. And even if my health completely returned, I would be different." Hearing her express this sentiment wasn't a shock, as we'd been talking about the concept for a few days already. Yet seeing those words on the screen gave them a sense of finality, a new reality wrapped in a public declaration that she was forever altered by the sorrows that had befallen her. This was not a detour; it was a new path altogether.

In one poignant scene from *The Return of the King*, road-weary Frodo turns to Gandalf to lament the cost of his journey: "There is no real going back. Though I may come to the Shire, it will not seem the same; for I shall not be the same. I am wounded with knife, sting, and tooth, and a long burden. Where shall I find rest?"[2]

Whether your loved one is your spouse, your child, or another relation, they will change before your very eyes. The specifics of this transformation vary from person to person, dictated by different personalities and different stories. They may turn from being passionate to being passive, or from being tranquil to being stormy. They may display significant symptoms of traumatization or cognitive diminishment. They may experience all kinds of unwanted physiological changes due to symptoms, procedures, and medications. They may struggle spiritually in ways that were foreign to their walk with God before their path turned dark.

Your life patterns with them will likewise be altered. Shared activities are part of relationship building and usually form the backdrop for our enjoyment of other people. Chronic pain and illness can quickly steal away all manner of shared interests. Pain may preclude exercise. Dietary restrictions can sideline exploring new foods or eating anything beyond the blandest of diets. Motor hindrances may make model building impossible. If your loved one is your spouse, your patterns of physical intimacy may be significantly changed, as I discuss in appendix B.

All these losses are points of sorrow. Our interests are our interests because we enjoy them. At the same time, these losses challenge us to come to terms with whether we truly love the other person or only love them for the happiness they're able to produce in us. Love that only loves someone else for what they can do for us isn't real love. Jesus reminds us of this in one of his sermons:

> If you love those who love you, what credit is that to you? Even sinners love those who love them. If you do what is good to those who are good to you, what credit is that to you? Even sinners do that. (Luke 6:32–33)

Our love for our loved one is most proven when they aren't able to do or be what we wish they were or used to be, as true love loves the real person.

I have had to learn how to find in this new version of Kate the things that I enjoyed about the old Kate. My wife has always had a never-say-die personality. She played an entire season of softball on a torn ACL because she loved the sport too much to be bothered to get surgery. It's discombobulating to see this same woman struggle to walk some days. A wise counselor helped me to realize that she still possesses her old grit and determination, only now she expresses it by completing what would otherwise be the mundane happenings of life. She gets out of bed and helps the kids with homework. She uses her gifts as a counselor and an artist. Those activities were easy for her before. Now they require a herculean effort many days. My eyes have needed to become sharper, more attuned to pick out the pattern of her character in the drab background of a chronic pain life.

You may resonate with this, or you may be in a situation where the person your loved one once was has faded entirely. Traumatic brain injuries, encephalitis, Alzheimer's, ALS, and a host of other chronic conditions may extinguish your loved one's spark and personality. This loss is grievous, one that human beings were not designed to endure. If this is your calling, there's no point of shame in weeping as you pick up this cross and follow Jesus. You exhibit a beautiful love, a love rooted in self-giving commitment. The Lord has promised that "you will receive the reward of an inheritance" from him one day (Col. 3:24). Future promises don't eliminate current sorrow, but one day that heavy burden will be lifted and all those tears wiped away.

NAVIGATING NEW RELATIONAL STREETS

When our family moved last year, Kate and I inherited a whole new set of roads to memorize—and with that came a whole new set of potholes to remember. Drive on a set of roads enough times and navigating around the jarring bits becomes second nature. I don't have to think, "Scoot right after the Dollar General, as there's a big divot to avoid." I just do it instinctively. But move to a new area, and I have to memorize a whole new map of road hazards that need to be avoided.

As you and your loved one both change, new potholes will appear and will need to be mapped in your relationship. Trying to live how you used to live is a recipe for getting quickly knocked out of alignment. You will both need to embrace transparency, honesty, durability, and kindness as you discuss the ways that life has changed.[3]

Kate and I decided when we married to invest our time in the things that we enjoyed doing together. I stopped watching sports and playing disc golf, and she pulled back on her art and animals. None of these were bad things. We just preferred to spend the time doing things we both enjoyed.

Chronic pain and illness have completely rewritten that plan. Kate spends large amounts of time in her craft room, making beautiful art with the energy she has. I spend a lot of time running on trails and open roads. She needs to feel like she's still creating things that make the world a more beautiful place; I need to be able to challenge myself and de-stress. We don't spend nearly the same amount of time together that we did before. It's not unfaithfulness; it's just that the relationship has changed.

All along the way we've needed to stay in honest dialogue with each other. I've had to learn to speak up and say, "I feel like things related to your health are overwhelming, and I need a little time to breathe and just be me." There are also times that Kate has come to me and said, "I feel like you're prioritizing yourself over me and our family right now." We map that pothole and work to bring life back into alignment. These conversations aren't always easy and may take several days to work through sometimes, but the temporary bumpiness of dealing with issues is far better for our relational health than ignoring them and hoping they just go away.

These conversations aren't restricted to what we do in our free time but happen across all aspects of life. They require a great deal of trust in each other. How does Kate know that when I say I need a breather, I'm not just being lazy? And how do I know that when she needs more of my attention she's not being self-centered? We trust each other because we've both demonstrated that we're for each other. We've used a fair amount of discretionary funds on her passion projects. I prioritize being at her doctor's appointments. She creates space for me to write and travel to teach. Love and trust cover a multitude of jarring moments when your relational right tire discovers a new pothole.[4]

YOUR RELATIONSHIP WITH OTHERS

Chronic pain and illness will also change your relationships with those outside your immediate family. One of my personal and professional heroes is the author and counselor David Powlison. His life was derailed by chronic fatigue that lasted for five years after his open-heart surgery. He remembers, "Fatigue destroyed much of my life. . . . I had to let go of many things that were valuable, gratifying, and joyous. My social circle became smaller and smaller, finally narrowing down to family and a few friends."[5]

Last week I spent fourteen hours on doctor's appointments, health research, bill paying, and other medical-related challenges. Caretaking and advocacy are no small endeavors. Some weeks that number is higher, while other weeks it is lower. You may inhabit these roles 168 hours a week, 52 weeks a year. All these hours have to come from somewhere. We are all finite human beings, with limited supplies of time and energy.

As you walk this road, some relationships will fall to the wayside, starved out by a famine of time. Others may spring up, forged in the fires of shared experiences. And at other times you may have to make a conscious decision to part with friends who do not adapt well to the new realities of your life. Kate and I have both experienced all three of these movements, for blessing and for sorrow.

Relationships That Grow

One of the individuals this book is dedicated to is Jeremy Wright, a pastor, friend, and fellow chronic illness spouse. The other day we were talking about how both of us (and our spouses) have developed ears that can typically tell when a preacher has experienced deep, soul-bending suffering. Jeremy remarked that "there's an accent that tells us you're from our town or that you're not from around these parts."[6] There's less bravado and more mercy for those living through the real struggles of life. There's more weakness and fewer lofty stories about martyrdom.

Jeremy has been a gift to me as a friend. Our realities are similar, and we don't need to explain ourselves to each other. C. S. Lewis famously wrote that "friendship arises . . . when two or more . . . companions discover that they have in common some insight or interest or even taste which the others do not share and which, till that moment, each believed to be his own unique treasure (or burden). The typical expression of opening Friendship would be something like, 'What? You too? I thought I was the only one.'"[7]

While having a friend who walks the same road has been helpful, chronic pain and illness are not the only way to develop a suffering-tinged accent. Someone whose infant child died of SIDS may not be able to picture exactly what it's like for you as you work through your husband's early-onset dementia. You won't necessarily connect exactly with someone who has experienced pervasive discrimination based upon their ethnicity or economic bracket. But those who have not just tasted but drunk deeply of the bitterness of this earth hold deep sorrow in common.

Those brothers and sisters are part of God's gift to you. The apostle Paul puts his own experience of the relationship of sufferers this way:

> [God] comforts us in all our affliction, so that we may be able to comfort those who are in any kind of affliction, through the comfort we ourselves receive from God. . . . If we are afflicted, it is for your comfort and salvation. If we are comforted, it is for your comfort, which produces in you patient endurance of the same sufferings that we suffer. (2 Cor. 1:4, 6)

Sometimes we hastily put ourselves in the place of the apostle Paul, feeling pressure to be able to comfort others. But I would encourage you to first identify as a receiver rather than a giver. God offers you his comfort through those whom he has drawn along hard paths as well. Finding and investing in those relationships is finding and investing in God's help for you as you walk a difficult path. Whether in the local church, in support groups, or in friendships that just naturally arise, fellow Christians who have felt sorrows and scars can support your weary arms and strengthen your tired heart.

Navigating Challenging Relationships

I had the honor to attend an event featuring a missionary who had been held captive and tortured for two years. This man spoke movingly of facing weakness and doubt during his captivity. The first question from the audience came from an elderly woman: "I saw a picture of you meeting with and praying for our president. Wouldn't you say it was all worth it for you to be able to pray for him in person?" Describing the silence after that question as "awkward" would be a significant understatement. He responded graciously, especially for a man whose experience of being separated from his family and tortured had just been overlooked in favor of politics.

By all appearances, this woman was a faithful follower of Christ, and given our location in the American South, probably a veteran of many church prayer chains, Bible studies, and meal trains. And I think that if someone had come alongside her after the event and said, "Let me tell you what everyone else just heard when you asked that question," she would have been mortified at how her words came across. We all tend to be tone-deaf to how we're perceived and tone-aware to how others' words land on us.

If you've walked the path of chronic pain and illness for long, you've undoubtedly been the recipient of many unhelpful comments and suggestions. People unhelpfully toss Bible verses around as little more than trite slogans. Your experience of sorrow gets labeled as a threat to true godliness. Acquaintances wax poetic about miracle cures and press you to just see this doctor or pursue that treatment if you really want healing.

Most of the time people who say the wrong thing have no clue they're being unhelpful. Should they be better than they are? Yes. Whether from a cultural discomfort with suffering, an inability to put themselves in someone else's shoes, or simple forgetfulness to listen first and talk second, the unhelpful, unkind, and sometimes cruel things people say or do cause real harm.

It's not wrong for you to be frustrated by such things. There will be times when you whisper to yourself, "God, rescue me from other people's good intentions." And yet you and I also must be patient with others, knowing that we too are limited, finite human beings who struggle to see perspectives beyond our own.

It's for moments when we are aggrieved that the apostle Paul wrote,

> Put on compassion, kindness, humility, gentleness, and patience, bearing with one another and forgiving one another if anyone has a grievance against another. (Col. 3:12–13)

A biblical scholar once told me that "bearing with one another" might be better translated as "putting up with each other." The second rendering is rougher, less church-like. But I think it captures well the realities of life as relational beings in this post-Eden world.

Bearing with other people is often the most Christlike response to their lack of consideration. However, there are times when kindness means helping someone else see better ways to care for you as you're hurting. In those moments when you weigh whether to speak or be silent, consider the following three questions as helpful guides:

- *Am I the right person to say something?* The closer your relationship to someone, the more you should be willing to speak up. Friendships are designed to be mutually edifying so that we can help one another grow.
- *Is now the right time to say something?* Your goal is to win your friend or family member over, not to humiliate or hurry them. Such conversations are good to have in private, with enough time to make sure you understand each other and are able to ask questions.
- *Am I in a good place right now to say something?* Let's be honest—the words that tumble out of you when you're hurt by something someone else has done will rarely help

others. Have conversations when you're able to clearly and calmly discuss what has hurt you and how to move forward.

Conversations like these are sometimes risky. Some people are quick to hear, but others may react with defensiveness or hurt that you would accuse them of being uncaring. The sobering truth is that you're on a new path, and not everybody will have the relational and emotional range to walk this craggy road with you. There are times that you'll need to make a conscious choice to take a step back from a relationship when a person demonstrates that they are persistently harmful. Your primary relational calling is to your loved one, and sometimes love for them may compel you to place a relationship to the side.

7

CLOUD OF WITNESSES

My first ultramarathon went badly. I suffered a hip injury early on, leading to a race that was two hours of fun followed by almost six hours of hobbling and pain management. By mile twenty I was in a pretty dark place. Every step hurt like crazy, and I still had more than a third of the race to go. As I was wallowing in my self-imposed misery, a train of three men ran past me. The expletives flying from their mouths were a tip-off that they were miserable too, but they were moving better than I was.

I made the painful decision to hook myself to the end of their line and follow in their footsteps. When they ran, I ran. When they slowed to hike a hill, I slowed. When they paused for water or food, I paused. They set the pace for me for several miles, taking away the need for me to think and allowing me to just focus on putting one foot in front of another. Eventually I couldn't keep up anymore, and they disappeared around a bend in the trail.

I finished that race only ten minutes before the cutoff time. As a volunteer handed me the finisher's medal, I realized I wouldn't have made it in time without those three men. Following them gave me strength when I had none, and the ten minutes I saved by running instead of hiking was the difference between success and failure.

I think about those moments on the trail as I followed those other three runners more than I ever would have guessed. In many ways, it's become my mental image of the necessity of journeying with others on the path you and I walk. The author of the book of Hebrews writes something important for us:

> Therefore, since we also have such a large cloud of witnesses surrounding us, let us lay aside every hindrance and the sin that so easily ensnares us. Let us run with endurance the race that lies before us, keeping our eyes on Jesus, the pioneer and perfecter of our faith. (Heb. 12:1–2)

We are on a journey that may feel isolating, but we are surrounded by an often-unseen cloud of others. Many of them have finished their journey and now cheer on those of us still running (or more likely hobbling) along the difficult path.

In this chapter, I'm going to introduce you to four people who I have found to be friendly faces on the journey. I've never met any of them, but their stories have given my heart strength and confidence that it's possible to hike this path and make it to the end. Maybe you're not ready yet to bear the pain of reading about someone else's pain. If so, that's okay. Don't feel the need to rush things. Feel free to skip over this chapter. But if you're ready and able to hear from other people's stories, I now turn you over to B. B. Warfield, William McKinley, and the Friesens.[1]

B. B. WARFIELD

Benjamin Breckenridge (or "B. B." as he's known) Warfield (1851–1921) was a stalwart systematic theology professor at Princeton Theological Seminary. His most enduring work, *The Inspiration and Authority of Scripture*, was a monumental book defending the perfection and truthfulness of Scripture during a time when many began describing the Bible as a human book full of errors.

To describe Warfield as "well-known" is to undersell his fame, at least for a theology professor. Invitations to speak at churches and theological conferences poured into his office at Princeton, invitations that he consistently declined. Indeed, for ten years the man known as the "Lion of Princeton" didn't leave his house for more than two hours at a time.

Professors have long been known for their eccentricities, but it was not brilliance bordering on oddity that led Warfield to such behavior. It was his ailing wife, Annie. Warfield married Annie Kinkead in 1876 at the age of twenty-five, and the newlyweds sailed for Leipzig, Germany, for a yearlong honeymoon and study abroad. One day the Warfields were caught in a tremendous thunderstorm in the mountains, an event that seems to have had a significant impact upon Annie's health for the rest of her life. Some reports have her being struck by lightning. While this appears to be more myth than truth, something seems to have happened that had long-term repercussions for Annie's health.

The snapshots we have of their early years show them enjoying a normal life: hosting parties for students, taking excursions into Pennsylvania's Pocono Mountains for holidays, and traveling three hundred miles back home to Kentucky for Christmas. Eight years into their marriage, Annie accompanied her husband on a major trip to Ireland and England for the Pan Presbyterian Council.

Yet dark storm clouds were ominously building on the horizon for B. B. and Annie. B. B. notes that the trip to the British Isles was "difficult" for Annie. Four years later, a note appears in a letter to a friend that she's sick and in need of consistent nursing. By the early 1890s, the word *invalid* begins to be scattered throughout the family's correspondence. She would rally at points, but her health's trajectory pointed ever downward.

Annie was rarely seen outside her own house during the last ten years of her life. Trips turned into walks, walks turned into being homebound, and being homebound turned into remaining bedridden. Warfield would walk across campus, teach his classes, and return home to his ailing wife. Far from being resentful over the way his wife's illness hindered his career, B. B. was well-known for his deep love for Annie. Upon her death in 1915, a colleague remarked that "[B. B.] has had only two interests in life—his work, and Mrs. Warfield, and now that she is gone there may be danger of his using himself up rather quickly."[2] Five years later B. B. joined his wife with the Lord, and his body was buried next to hers under matching bronze crosses to await the final resurrection.

IF I WERE ABLE TO SIT DOWN to a cup of tea with B. B. Warfield, I would love to ask him about how he handled having his professional career significantly reshaped by his wife's health. Admittedly, I'm drawn to B. B.'s story because of our shared vocation, yet there's something encouraging for all of us in the way he prioritized his wife over other opportunities.

B. B. lived during a time when the doctrine of Scripture was a point of serious discussion. Many denominations were beginning to describe the Bible as being a good book but one that was written only by humans and full of historical errors. Warfield defended the orthodox position that the Bible is God's inspired, inerrant Word, and this work led to significant opportunities. Who better to steam across the ocean and defend the truthfulness of the Bible in the greatest schools in Europe than the Lion of Princeton?

I wonder how often he was tempted to hire a caregiver, declare the Battle for the Bible to be more important than caring for his ailing wife, and pursue the opportunities that so many people offered him. I can't be sure, but if Warfield is anything like you and me, he must have experienced moments of sadness, anger, and frustration when he was unable to do what any of his colleagues could have freely done.

If there's one thing for you to learn from Warfield at this moment, it's to devote yourself to the things that only you can do. There were others who could go and defend God's Word. They may not have had as cool a nickname as "the Lion of Princeton," but they could faithfully and persuasively speak on the theological topics of the day. Annie Warfield had only one husband. And only he could love her, be with her, and prioritize her.

We will have all kinds of opportunities in life. While these probably won't include speaking at international conferences, there will be the opportunity to accept that promotion at work requiring you to travel more. There will be chances to volunteer with that charity. There will be the opportunity to coach a sport. Whatever your particular lane is, put it here.

Faithfulness doesn't require turning all these down, but it does mean asking yourself the question "What does it look like to prioritize the things that only I can do?" Loving your diminished family member or friend is rarely flashy. Your acts of kindness and faithfulness toward them will likely never be seen by others.

I once attended a school that had William Carey's famous slogan emblazoned on the wall when you entered a main door: "Expect great things from God. Attempt great things for God." This is a wonderful rallying cry. But often those great things are not the things that are thought of as being great in the eyes of the world (or even in the eyes of many Christians). Greatness isn't counted by God as numbers or influence. It's counted as being faithful to however he has decided to shape your life. He is the potter, and you're the clay. Sometimes greatness looks like changing a bedpan. Sometimes greatness looks like wheeling a wheelchair. Sometimes greatness looks like listening to your loved one process what has befallen them yet again. Those unseen moments are holy before God, and he sees in them true greatness.

WILLIAM MCKINLEY

William McKinley is little more than an afterthought on most lists of great presidents. Even though he presided over a momentous time in American history, McKinley himself is most remembered for his last act as the chief executive—dying at the hands of an assassin's bullet while attending the Pan-American Exposition in Buffalo, New York.

McKinley was a measured, contemplative man. And while his public life may not inspire future generations to great deeds, his personal life reveals a man of greatness. Staid William married the energetic and well-educated Ida Saxon on January 25, 1871, in Canton, Ohio. Ida was quite the catch for the young lawyer. Before marrying William, she had traveled throughout Europe, becoming involved in improving the working conditions of poor seamstresses in the lace industry. She earned the equivalent of a master of fine arts and became a manager at her father's bank—both almost unheard of for a woman in mid-nineteenth-century America. One biographer captures well the couple's relational dynamics: "On one side was a sober, excessively polite, somewhat prudish lawyer who kept his emotions always in check. On the other was an impulsive, witty, flirtatious young woman with an appetite for adventure and rollicking times. But he was thoroughly captivated by her lively wholesomeness, expansive intellect, and underlying sound judgment, and she appreciated his rectitude, kind regard for others, and smoldering ambition."[3]

The McKinleys rejoiced at the birth of two daughters within the first three years of their marriage. Tragically, both succumbed to illness, with little Ida (named for her mother) living less than five months and little Katie passing away shortly before her fifth birthday.

These twin griefs were coupled with a serious accident that injured Ida's spine and hindered her ability to walk, causing significant impact to her well-being. Ida's health became a story woven through William's rise to becoming the governor of Ohio and then the president.

Ida began suffering from seizures and found herself unable to participate in the physical activities that punctuated her life before injury and loss. Most seizure patients were removed to insane asylums in that era, as seizures were considered a sign of madness and not a true medical condition, but William "resolved to nurture [Ida] through life and through the matrix of maladies that had descended upon her with such menace."[4]

This commitment to his wife transformed how McKinley pursued his political career. His opponent for president in 1896 was the silver-tongued orator William Jennings Bryan. Bryan possessed boundless energy in addition to his rhetorical polish, and he traveled over eighteen thousand miles by rail during his campaign. In completing this astonishing feat, Bryan sought to capture the imaginations of voters who had previously needed to be content with reading about presidential candidates in their hometown newspapers.[5]

McKinley faced significant pressure to match his rival's barnstorming strategy, driven by the well-founded fear that a man who was willing to visit voters in their own towns would be more compelling than one not disposed to make such a trip. Ida's health precluded a cross-country train ride, and McKinley was entirely unwilling to abandon his ailing wife for months in pursuit of the presidency. He ran a "front porch" campaign from a house in Canton, inviting voters from across the United States to come and see him.

The hard-fought presidential campaign came down to the wire, and McKinley proved triumphant. His elevation to the highest office in the land invited fresh eyes to be placed on the McKinleys, not all of which looked with favor on the chronically ill First Lady. The wife of one Texas congressman recorded in her journal, "[The] first glimpse of Mrs. McKinley made me feel ashamed of coming.... [The] poor, suffering woman ... ought to have been hidden from the gaze of the curious."[6] These private remarks were published not long after their penning.

If you run an internet search for Ida McKinley, you'll be greeted by her official White House biography. Even today, how she's remembered now is hardly an improvement over those shameful words written so long ago by her contemporaries: "There was little resemblance between the vivacious young woman who married William McKinley in January 1871 . . .

and the petulant invalid who moved into the White House with him in March 1897. Now her face was pallid and drawn, her close-cropped hair gray; her eyes were glazed with pain or dulled with sedative."[7]

McKinley was not deaf to the injurious comments directed toward his wife, yet he refused to cater to those who viewed her as a liability. He broke with over a century of tradition by placing Ida next to him during formal state dinners, a place previously reserved for dignitaries. He canceled speaking engagements, ended meetings, and altered formal events whenever her health demanded his attention.[8] Many members of his staff felt he doted on her excessively, but William called such attention love.

Both McKinleys were committed Christians, a fact on full display after bullets tore through William's clothing in New York. Recognizing the seriousness of his condition, he turned to his assistant, George Cortelyou, and urged, "My wife—be careful . . . how you tell her—oh, be careful."[9] The president lingered for a few days before it became clear his end was drawing near. He asked for Ida, reminded her that one day they would be together again, and recited the popular hymn "Nearer My God to Thee."[10] After William's passing, Ida returned to Canton, where she lived with family and visited her husband's grave almost daily until her own passing six years later.[11]

SHOULD I BE ABLE to refill my cup and sit down with William McKinley, I would love to hear more about his willingness to elevate his wife at the cost of ridicule to himself. McKinley was a man who would rather offend dignitaries and disappoint voters than leave his wife out.

If you've walked the chronic pain and illness road for long, you've undoubtedly felt some version of this particular trouble.

Individuals whose health places them outside the norm can tend to attract eyeballs and evaluations in ways that are uncomfortable. This is especially the case if your loved one's health causes observable symptoms. Wheelchairs, oxygen tanks, slurred speech, cognitive impairment, socially unusual behavior—all of them can attract unwanted attention.

My wife's health struggles do not produce symptoms that are noticeable at a glance. I can tell when she's struggling, but that's through knowing a particular look in her eyes and pattern in her speech. Most people have no clue unless she tells them.

Even with the lack of publicly observable symptoms, I've had to grow in my ability and willingness to shrug off potential societal embarrassment for the sake of my wife. This may sound silly to you, but one of the chief places I struggle with this is at church. Mornings are a challenge for Kate, and oftentimes making it to even the last service at our church can be difficult. My heart whispers that it's not a good look for the counseling minister to be one of the last cars pulling into the parking lot week after week, walking through the doors as the worship team finishes its first (or second) set.

What about for you, friend? In what ways do you find discomfort, embarrassment, or frustration creeping up inside of you due to your loved one's sufferings? When do you find yourself thinking, "I wonder what they think of us?" Such thoughts are almost inevitable—the main question is what we will do with them when they happen. William McKinley encourages us to worry less about what others think and worry more about prioritizing the ones we've promised to love. If he can do it as president, then surely you or I can bear up under the load of others' unhelpful assumptions in our far more modest spheres.

DOUG AND LISA FRIESEN

The third family populating our cloud of witnesses does not have the same name recognition as the Warfields or McKinleys. Doug and Lisa Friesen live lives that are far closer to yours and mine than those of White House residents or cutting-edge theologians. The Friesens are largely unknown outside their small circle in northern Illinois, where they have resided for more than twenty-five years.

Two decades ago, the Friesens' daughter, Katelyn, was suddenly beset by significant anxiety and depression. The strength of these difficulties was unusual for an eight-year-old girl with a generally happy and stable life. Even stranger were the times she would hallucinate about home intruders. Doctor after doctor pointed to these symptoms as rooted in mental health troubles, but no amount of counseling, medication, or other treatments improved her experience.

Sadly, Katelyn became the target of bullying at school, and this in conjunction with her unshakeable depression and anxiety led to a downward spiral of destructive choices. She began cutting and purging, and eventually the thoughts of self-harm and suicide became so pervasive that she spent more time inside of the hospital than outside.

Doug and Lisa checked Katelyn into a recommended Christian residential facility where she could receive around-the-clock specialized care. What seemed like a godsend, however, turned out to be a place of torment. Katelyn and other residents were subjected to physical mistreatment and severe manipulation. Staff tried to undermine Katelyn's relationship with her parents, insisting that if they really loved her and wanted her, they would not have left her there. In the end, the place that had once promised so much hope left a legacy of devastation as it closed under the specter of criminal investigations.

In the years since Katelyn escaped that facility, her health has continued to deteriorate. What doctors first described as mental health issues were suddenly joined by other issues such as neurological-gastrointestinal trouble, asthma, and postural orthostatic tachycardia syndrome (POTS). She experiences up to ten seizures a day, with paralysis sometimes lasting days afterward. A question that puzzled doctors remained unanswered: Is this a collection of separate problems, or is there a yet-to-be-found door that, when unlocked, will tie all these disparate symptoms together?

One day doctors found the key. Katelyn was diagnosed with bartonellosis—a bacterial infection that is contracted through certain types of insect bites. Anxiety, depression, and hallucinations are known symptoms, as are the physical problems that she has developed more recently. Two decades' worth of medication, therapies, and counseling were all ineffective because they had targeted the wrong thing. The problem wasn't mental or spiritual; it was a bug bite. After the diagnosis, Doug and Lisa thought back to a family vacation right before her first symptoms arose. While playing in the backyard, Katelyn was savagely bitten by insects to such an extent that she had to be taken to urgent care because of the swelling.

Despite the diagnosis, Katelyn's health struggles continue. Lisa chose to leave a job she loved in order to be available to pursue the care Katelyn needs. It's unclear how much of Katelyn's current struggles are due to bartonellosis or to decades of wrongly focused treatments. The Friesens live in the tension between joy over finding a cause and sorrow over wondering what might have been had diagnosis come sooner.

Danish philosopher and theologian Søren Kierkegaard once wrote in his journal that "life can only be understood backwards; but it must be lived forwards."[12] While he probably wasn't thinking about the pursuit of a medical diagnosis, his words capture well the frustration of having little clarity in the midst of chronic pain and illness.

THE FRIESENS' STORY ILLUSTRATES the painful truth that medical choices aren't always clear. We wrestle with questions that may have long-term effects upon our loved ones. Will this procedure hurt or help? Is this use of money wise or foolish? Are the risks worth the possible reward? Even when we pray and sit and trust God to guide us, his guidance doesn't always lead us to solutions. In the haze, we follow doctors down wrong paths and make choices that in retrospect are regrettable.

Diagnosis may bring the joy of answers, but it can also invite the unwanted houseguests of regret, guilt, and anger to take up residence in the heart. How could we have been so foolish? Why didn't the doctors run that test? How dare insurance delay and deny something until it was too late? Could I have researched more, fought harder, driven just a bit further to that other specialist?

The Friesens' story reminds us of the hard truth that living as people limited in knowledge is often a rough go. We can't know the outcomes of the paths we take until we've walked them. We can't know how much the path may further break us and our loved ones. We worship a God who does, but he's also a God who makes no promises about steering us toward solutions to physical problems.

Instead, he offers us something better. He promises that all sorrow and suffering will be met with his supernatural comfort.

He promises that beauty will come from ashes and that one day the path will make sense once we see things from a peak high atop a mountain in the new heavens and new earth. It doesn't always feel better. There are days that guilt, regret, and anger threaten to swallow up such a vision. But the Friesens remind you and me that God's goodness and mercy follow us and that we can trust him even when the road behind is full of wrong paths and dead ends.[13]

I NEED THESE STORIES, AND YOU NEED THESE STORIES

You and I need these kinds of stories. Isolation and hopelessness often walk hand in hand. We're far more vulnerable to the roaring, devouring lion when we've lost sight of our herd: God's people who have walked where we walk. The real stories of others can be companions from God for our encouragement and our protection.

8

THE END

We've reached the final chapter of this little book. I hope it has been helpful for you, even as it has been helpful (though at times painful) for my heart to write. Since this is the final chapter, we need to talk about the end.

The end is coming for us all, isn't it? The author of Hebrews confirms what we all know, reminding us "it is appointed for people to die" (Heb. 9:27). Ever-cheerful Quoleth chimes in more poetically: "It is better to go to a house of mourning than to go to a house of feasting, since that is the end of all mankind, and the living should take it to heart" (Eccl. 7:2).

The moment our lungs filled with breath for the first time, we entered into a bargain in which one day those same lungs will deflate for the last time. God tells us to consider this fact and to concern ourselves not just with living but also with dying.

The troubles and questions and sorrows of the chronic pain and illness affecting life don't simply stand down when it comes to thinking about the end. Considering your end can throw you into a tumble. Death may sound inviting, a blessed release from the pressure and anxiety and sorrows of your life. Or it may be a source of anxiety driven by worry over what would happen to your loved one (and potentially other family members) should your earthly life come to a close before theirs. You could experience a whiplash-inducing blend of the two, mixed in with general numbness and a fear that you'll die angry at the God you're about to meet.

Thinking about the end is rarely clean for human beings, and even less so when the realities of chronic pain and illness get layered on top of an already complicated topic.

THE TREE

Every time you see your loved one, you see a witness to the fact that we are not yet living in the world where all will be made new. Your weary hands, anxiety-driven insomnia, and sorrow over missing what could have been all nod along in unison with the testimony of your loved one's body.

Many ancient Greek philosophers considered the frailness of the human body and concluded that perfection must involve throwing off their ever-limiting meat sacks and living as free, unbounded spirit. But God's version of a perfected human being is surprisingly different. In his plan, he takes our bodies—those sources of so much struggle and pain—and causes them to spring back to life at the call of their Creator. He reshapes and refashions them into bodies that work the way they were intended to work. Nerves do not grow angry and scream into our brains. Chromosomes are not missing as the body consults its internal blueprint. Our immune systems do not suddenly declare war on our own healthy tissues.

Way back in Genesis 2, before the unmaking of the world, God placed Adam and Eve in his beautiful garden. At its center was the Tree of Life, alongside the Tree of the Knowledge of Good and Evil. This second tree ensnared Eve and then Adam, who were then punished by God for eating of its fruit in disobedience to him. Being cast out from Eden meant being cut off from the Tree of Life. Moses records God's thoughts for us: "Since the man has become like one of us, knowing good and evil, he must not reach out, take from the tree of life, eat, and live forever" (Gen. 3:22).

After this grim declaration, the Tree of Life disappears as a plot point from the Bible.

The patriarchs are built into the nation of Israel. God's people are led out from Egypt, build a great civilization, fall into spiritual ruin, and are conquered and deported. The Savior comes, the church is built, and nary a word is spoken about the tree that was lost to the human race. Then suddenly, in the final book of the entire Bible, it reappears. It's the overlooked minor character of a novel who turns out to play an essential part in the resolution of the whole story.[1]

It is the Lord himself who first reminds us of this tree, so long ago forgotten after being shut up in a garden guarded by angels. He whispers that "to the one who conquers, I will give the right to eat from the tree of life, which is in the paradise of God" (Rev. 2:7). This whisper grows in strength as he clearly voices what joy the tree of life can bring: "The leaves of the tree are for healing the nations, and there will no longer be any curse" (Rev. 22:2–3). Remember this curse? It's the one that promised that suffering and pain would be part and parcel of the human experience. It's the one that promised that "in this life you will have trouble." Although there are no healing trees shading the land we now live in, the Bible's final chapter assures us that one day we will walk beside one again.

I don't know if this is a literal tree planted in the middle of the new earth. John's book is full of images because he's written in a genre that isn't remembered much anymore: apocalypse. Apocalyptic literature is designed to make you feel things. It communicates truth, but you don't press apocalypses for exacting details; you press them for feelings. How do you feel when you hear of a dragon that sweeps a third of the stars from the sky? How do you feel when you think of a tree unfolding its luxurious leaves and binding up the nations' wounds, wiping away their tears? That's the point that John wants you to walk away with.

Maybe it's a real tree; maybe it's an image. But remember that the purpose of Revelation is to evoke in us the feelings we would feel if we stumbled into a walled garden after a long journey and found the one tree whose fruit would refresh us to the uttermost. Theologian Tom Schreiner captures the point behind the images: "No one in the new creation gets sick and stands in need of healing; the tree of life and its healing properties point to the perfect shalom [peace] and health present in the new Jerusalem."[2]

What does this mean? It means that as surely as you live and breathe today, one day pain will no longer carve its way through the nervous system of your loved one who knows the Lord.[3] It means that cells will not wildly multiply out of control into cancer and that muscles and bones will not be hollowed out with unexplainable or untreatable weakness.

And for you, the leaves of this tree will heal your worries and your grief and your sorrow that you have carried faithfully until that day. No more late-night vigils. No more questions and confusion. No more doctor visits tearing holes in your schedule, bank account, relationships, and heart. It will all be done away with, passed into the rearview mirror of a road already traveled. God's presence offers you comfort and light and rest:

Look, God's dwelling is with humanity, and he will live with them. They will be his peoples, and God himself will be with them and will be their God. He will wipe away every tear from their eyes. Death will be no more; grief, crying, and pain will be no more, because the previous things have passed away. (Rev. 21:3–4)

Storytellers have long tried to capture this joy. C. S. Lewis's remade Narnia crackles with energy as the Pevensies and Narnians alike race through the familiar-yet-new landscape.[4] Peter Jackson's movie version of *The Lord of the Rings* lets us overhear a conversation between the wise wizard-guide Gandalf and the little hobbit Pippin, who is distressed over his own likely death in the coming battle, in which the forces of good are hopelessly outnumbered:

PIPPIN: I didn't think it would end this way.

GANDALF: End? No, the journey doesn't end here. Death is just another path, one that we all must take. The grey rain-curtain of this world rolls back, and all turns to silver glass, and then you see it.

PIPPIN: What? Gandalf? See what?

GANDALF: White shores, and beyond, a far green country under a swift sunrise.

PIPPIN: Well, that isn't so bad.

GANDALF: No. No, it isn't.[5]

Rest, peace, joy, vigor, delight, happiness, satisfaction—this is the lexicon of where we will be. Gone are their opposites, wiped away by God himself, who now dwells with us as he did in Eden.

LIVING NOW, DREAMING OF THEN

Sometimes knowing my future gives me strength to continue serving my wife and family. As when I run a grueling race, I know that there is a finish line and that hard-earned rest will be mine once I cross that line. All I must do is keep putting one foot in front of the other, knowing that all this pain is temporary. And if it's temporary, it's endurable.

Other times, the promise that old tears will pass away is more mystifying than comforting. I know that good things await; however, that future experience of goodness doesn't entirely smooth over all my questions now. While there will be no more tears or crying or pain, we also won't get to go back and raise our kids with all the energy and clarity and gusto that we wish we had. We won't get to rewind the tape and live the marriage that we wanted. You won't get to have your child live a normal, carefree childhood and grow to adulthood. And that's perplexing. The future is bright, but present joys are slipping through your fingers, never to be felt again.

I can't say I have a neat and tidy answer for this trouble. I truly don't understand why God has allowed this into our lives. It might be the same for you. Time and again in the midst of tears about joy lost, Kate and I return to a simple truth. God doesn't ask us to understand his plan; he asks us for faith.

I don't know how the sorrows of this life will be entirely wiped away. I'm not sure I even comprehend how it's possible, given the sheer carnage of human suffering spanning from the opening of history until its end. How will there be no more tears for lives cut short? No sorrow over years stolen by chronic pain and illness?

When I am asking such questions, a stanza from an old song that was revived by a new tune during my college days often comes to mind. In it, the singer reminds their tired soul of essential truth:

> Soon shall close thy earthly mission
> Soon shall pass thy pilgrim days
> Hope shall change to glad fruition
> Faith to sight, and prayer to praise.[6]

My soul, and undoubtedly yours as well, is full of questions that don't entirely have answers. But we don't need answers. We need to trust God. One day our faith will be sight and our prayers of sorrow will turn to words of praise. And some way, somehow, the sorrows we have borne in this life will serve to magnify the joys of the next, as "this light momentary affliction is preparing for us an eternal weight of glory beyond all comparison" (2 Cor. 4:17 ESV).

COME, LORD JESUS!

When I was younger, I used to have more apprehension about the Lord's second coming. There were so many things I wanted to do in life: get married, have a family, do ministry, build a fulfilling career, explore the world, and complete a whole host of other things.

But now, having spent years in the land of shadows, I've come to understand the final cry in the book of Revelation: "Come, Lord Jesus!" (Rev. 22:20). Come, Lord Jesus, and bid troubles cease. Come, Lord Jesus, and let my loved one's pain cease. Come, Lord Jesus, and let this weariness be replaced with peace. Come, Lord Jesus, and may the constant hum of worry be replaced with security. Come, Lord Jesus, and let my questions and doubts be overshadowed by the pure radiance of walking with you. Come quickly, Lord Jesus.

The promise is fixed and real and certain. Our God has spoken our future to us already:

> Then the one seated on the throne said, "Look, I am making everything new." He also said, "Write, because these words are faithful and true." Then he said to me, "It is done! I am the Alpha and the Omega, the beginning and the end. I will freely give to the thirsty from the spring of the water of life." (Rev. 21:5–6)

And so, friend, I will end our conversation together the same way that I speak to my own heart. Your road may be dark and confusing and take you far beyond the end of your own strength. But don't give up too soon. One day you'll hear in your ears the words of your Savior, who, like you, is a survivor of deep trouble during his days on earth: "Well done, good and faithful servant" (Matt. 25:23).

I look forward to meeting you there.

ACKNOWLEDGMENTS

This book is simultaneously the most researched and least researched piece of writing I've ever completed. Kate Brooks and I have spent more than a decade wandering in the wilderness together, and what's written here is a product of the Spirit working in both our hearts as we've tripped over rocky outcroppings, cursed the blaring sun, and stumbled upon unexpected oases. Without her faith, her kindness, her wisdom, and her love, this book would never have been possible to write.

The draft version of this book was far inferior to the final copy. Talented and invested pre-readers are worth their weight in gold, and Jeremy and Alicia Wright, Jenny Solomon, and Kate Brooks increased my literary wealth greatly. Anna Mondal may not be a jeweler, but her wordsmithing took many rough-hued stones and made them shine. Thank you to all of you—your work made my work so much better.

Thank you as well to Dave Almack, Joy Woo, Amanda Martin, and the rest of the P&R team for shepherding this project from an idea to being a tiny part of the United States' GDP. I'm grateful for your keen insight into how to best frame concepts and ideas for maximum impact.

Acknowledgments

Thank you to my colleagues and the leadership of SEBTS for their support as I work unusual hours in the face of ever-shifting family commitments. They've covered classes so I can be at doctor's appointments, tolerated emails sent at inconvenient times, and been incredibly understanding as I've missed events due to family necessities. Working for an institution with that ethos means more than you all realize; thank you.

Thank you to Hozier, Fink, Chris Stapleton, and Julianna Barwick for providing the moody soundtrack this millennial needed to write a book on sorrow and hope.

Thank you to my father for providing an example of what it looked like to love a spouse whose life was interrupted by chronic health issues.

And last of all, I'm grateful for my children, whose character and graciousness continue to be honed by growing up in a home that they do not yet understand to be unusual. Blaise, Gresham, and Alethea, I know that Daddy writes totally unawesome books with no pictures, but may you find the greater land of which every earthly word and picture is but a hopeful shadow.

As always, no amount of faithful conversation, friendship, and editing would be sufficient to hold me back from all error, and whatever blemishes, errors, or untruths have seeped into this work are mine alone.

I pray you have been as blessed by reading this book as I have been in writing it.

Appendix A

FOR THE NON-CHRISTIAN READER

If you have picked up this book and aren't a Christian, I'm so glad that you're holding it in your hands. I respect you and the difficult path that you're walking as the loved one of someone suffering from chronic pain and illness. So many people give up and walk away, but choosing to stay proves you to be a person of character, fortitude, and love.

I don't know what you've made of the story I've told in this book. Maybe you think that I'm weak for needing religion as a crutch to survive. Maybe you've found some things appealing and want to know more. Maybe you tried Christianity once and were turned off by the people you found in church or some hard teachings from the Bible.

Wherever you're at, I do want you to hear me say that your life would be better with Christ than without him. We are all weak and frail, and living as the loved one of someone beset by chronic pain and illness highlights those weaknesses and frailties constantly. I hope you're able to hear that insufficiency as God tapping you on the shoulder, beckoning you to come and be with him.

The Bible is ultimately a story about reconciliation. We talked quite a bit about creation and the fall in the first few chapters of this book. God made us to be images of his character—beings full of beauty, truth, love, and perfection. Unfortunately, our first ancestors fell away from God and chose to rebel against his goodness. You and I and everyone else have followed this path; in the words of the Bible, "There is no one righteous, not even one. . . . All have turned away" (Rom. 3:10, 12).

I see the way that my own heart naturally strays from goodness every day. As I've mentioned before, I get angry when I shouldn't, operate out of selfishness, am an impatient father. Sure, I'm not the worst character out there. I meet with many men far worse than me in my counseling practice. But God doesn't evaluate us based on how good we are compared to others. He evaluates us based off what we should be, and that's absolute moral perfection. Being pretty good doesn't cut it.

Instead of condemning us all, God sent his Son to live the perfect life that we need to live and to die on a cross in our place. The Bible says that "the wages of sin is death, but the gift of God is eternal life in Christ Jesus our Lord" (Rom. 6:23). We need that perfect life Christ lived—a reality that undoubtedly you and I feel often as we carry this heavy burden.

How do we know that God is willing to accept Christ's life and death on our behalf? The wages of sin is death, and Christ's resurrection from the dead shows that God has accepted his sacrifice and that our debt has been paid in full.

There is one catch, however. God requires something from you and me to be given this great gift. The Bible describes it as "faith." Ephesians 2:8–9 says, "For you are saved by grace through faith, and this is not from yourselves; it is God's gift—not from works, so that no one can boast." This kind of faith is the deep trust that what God says about us is true, and it means placing all our hope in finding acceptance before God in Christ's work. It's not our doing good that makes us clean before God; it's Christ's goodness. And that can be ours through faith in Christ.

God promises that he'll give new hearts to those who place their faith in him. The old heart that rejects God is replaced by a new one that wants to follow him. We gain hearts that want to reach out to our loved ones in "love, joy, peace, patience, kindness, goodness, faithfulness, gentleness, and self-control" (Gal. 5:22–23). You will struggle with this, even as I have shared my struggles in this book. But God will draw your heart to his as you seek to follow him and ask for his help.

What I've just described is often called "the gospel." That's a Bible word that means "good news." Believing it isn't hard. It may hurt our pride, since we think we can do it on our own. It may offend our sense of being good. It will require us to change some things about how we live as God calls us to follow his Word, which is always for our good. But believing isn't hard. Jesus says to those of us who are worn out with grief and an endless mound of dishes, "Come to me, all of you who are weary and carry heavy burdens, and I will give you rest. . . . Let me teach you, because I am humble and gentle at heart, and you will find rest for your souls" (Matt. 11:28–29 NLT). As was talked about in the final chapter of this book, we get to taste that rest that God has promised now, but our final experience of it will be after we go to be with him. There all these tears will be wiped away, and we will see him face-to-face.

If you find yourself wanting to meet this Savior as a friend, talk to him about it. He can hear you. Confess that you're not enough and that you've tried to live your own way. Tell him about your sorrow for your sin and your desire to have his help. Tell him that you want a new heart and his help, and he will listen. If you're able, the next step is to find a community of other Christians. Look for a church that opens up the Bible and teaches what it says.

If you're not ready to take these steps, I understand. Life is challenging and confusing, and answers don't come easily. God wouldn't mind at all if you ask him to reveal himself to you, to help you see him. Whatever you choose, I just ask that you think more about this free offer of life. Notice where you fall short of your own standards and think about the help that's offered to you by the One who made you.

Appendix B

SEXUAL INTIMACY AND CHRONIC PAIN AND ILLNESS

A SECTION ON SEXUAL intimacy and chronic pain and illness would interrupt the flow of this book; however, I think it's an important enough topic to write a few extra words about at the end. God created us to delight in sex, and sex is one of the many joys that marriage affords.

Disruptions in a couple's sex life can be challenging to such a degree that Paul calls it a potential avenue by which Satan may attack you (1 Cor. 7:5). Your spouse is the one human being with whom you may have a sexual relationship, but when chronic pain and illness occur, your sexual preferences and patterns may be significantly impacted. This short appendix is in no way comprehensive or even thorough, but the following four thoughts and two next steps can help guide you and your spouse as you seek to navigate your new sexual normal.

Appendix B

Thought #1: Chronic pain and illness produce genuine suffering in your sex life with your spouse. Lament is a product of sorrow over loss, and you and your spouse are meant to lament your sexual losses. Take the time to name to God what you've lost, knowing that grief is a right and appropriate emotion.

Thought #2: The interruption to your sex life is a burden for your spouse as well. It may not seem like this at times. Sex may be far from their minds due to pain, but they would prefer to have a free and unhindered sex life with you. They may even feel guilty that their condition has led to sorrow and struggle for you.

Thought #3: Sex is a delight, but it is not a requirement for experiencing a full human life. Jesus did not have a sexual relationship, and many, many faithful Christians do not have sex lives due to singleness, widowhood, challenges with same-sex attraction, physical defects, and many other reasons. There's a reason why Song of Songs reminds us, "Do not stir up or awaken love until the appropriate time" (Song 8:4). It's challenging to have a sexual relationship and then put it on pause. However, God empowers you to say no to pornography, masturbation, fantasies, adultery, and other sexual sin.

Thought #4: Your role is to love your spouse well, and that means prioritizing their health over your sexual desires. If particular forms of sexual expression are painful for them, then don't do those things. If the category of sexuality is too taxing or troubling for them right now, patiently love them without pressuring them or making them feel guilty. To paraphrase the apostle Paul, do not destroy your spouse for the sake of sex (Rom. 14:20).

Step #1: If your relationship is safe and you're able to have open conversations about sex, work toward mutual understanding. It's good to grieve together the loss of something delightful, and it's also good to work together toward answering the question of what you *are* able to do together. You both are allies working alongside each other with love, patience, and kindness. Work together to identify what sexual actions you can do that express love and interest for each other. These should be pleasing to both of you, acceptable to your consciences, and honoring to God. Be patient with each other as you work to build a sex life that will look different from before. It will likely take time to figure out new patterns and approaches. Work together and think of this as a journey of discovery together.

Step #2: If this road of sexuality and chronic pain and illness is or remains confusing, consider meeting with a Christian counselor who is informed about trauma and chronic pain and who works with couples as they rebuild their sex lives. Such counselors can help you and your spouse communicate about sexuality better and creatively plan. If you're hesitant to talk about such intimate topics with someone, I'd encourage you to think about them in the same category as going to the doctor to talk about problems with your physical body. Like a good doctor, a good counselor treats such an intimate topic with dignity.

NOTES

Introduction
1. Salomon TV, "The Ultra Addict with Courtney Dauwalter," September 10, 2019, YouTube, https://www.youtube.com/watch?v=BbS32MAurnQ.

Chapter 1: When Suffering Isn't a Season
1. Dylan Thomas, "Do Not Go Gentle into That Good Night," in *In Country Sleep, and Other Poems* (New Directions, 1952).
2. C. S. Lewis, *The Lion, The Witch, and the Wardrobe* (repr., Collier, 1971), 16.

Chapter 2: I Didn't Sign Up for This
1. Cathy Crimmins, *Where Is the Mango Princess? A Journey Back from Brain Injury* (repr., Vintage, 2001), 3–4.
2. John Donne, "Meditation 17," in *Devotions upon Emergent Occasions* (London, 1624), 394–95.
3. J. R. R. Tolkien, *The Fellowship of the Ring* (Ballantine Books, 1965), 82.
4. B. B. Warfield, *The Emotional Life of Our Lord* (repr., Crossway, 2022), n.p. This work is widely available online.

Chapter 3: A Stranger in a Strange Land
1. This book cannot take a detour into the complex sociohistorical problem of poverty, crime, and ethnicity. For those wanting to study this topic more, I would recommend beginning with Shai

Linne's biblically grounded and experientially wise book *The New Reformation: Finding Hope in the Fight for Ethnic Unity* (Moody, 2021) and Isaac Adams's *Talking About Race: Gospel Hope for Hard Conversations* (Zondervan, 2022).
2. Thomas Hobbes, *Leviathan: The Matter, Forme, & Power of a Common-Wealth Ecclesiastical and Civill* (repr., The Floating Press, 2009), 179. This quotation has been slightly edited to update older English spellings.
3. John Piper, "Embrace the Life God Has Given You," March 10, 2017, YouTube, https://www.desiringgod.org/embrace-the-life-god-has-given-you.

Chapter 4: God, Interrupted

1. Bob Kellemen, "A Tale of Two Trusts: What Does It Mean to 'Suffer Well'?" RPM Ministries, January 31, 2021, https://rpmministries.org/2021/01/a-tale-of-two-trusts/.
2. Thomas O. Chisholm, "Great Is Thy Faithfulness," 1923.

Chapter 5: We Are Dust

1. Robert Robinson, "Come, Thou Fount of Every Blessing," 1758.
2. Timothy Keller, "Heman's Cry of Darkness," Gospel in Life, audio recording of a sermon given on November 4, 2007, https://gospelinlife.com/sermon/hemans-cry-of-darkness/.
3. Tremper Longman III, *Psalms: An Introduction and Commentary* (IVP Academic, 2014), 321.

Chapter 6: Renegotiating Relationships

1. "The Schmidt Sting Pain Index," The Natural History Museum, London, accessed May 15, 2024, https://www.nhm.ac.uk/scroller-schmidt-painscale/#15.
2. J. R. R. Tolkien, *The Return of the King* (Ballantine Books, 1965), 331.

3. Your loved one may not be able to have these kinds of conversations due to significant diminishment. If that's the case, then do the best you can, all while keeping love for your spouse central in your heart.
4. What I've written in this chapter assumes that you are in a relationship in which honesty and openness is safe. If you are in a relationship in which openness is unsafe or you find your loving honesty used against you, please consider talking to a counselor or advocate. Courage Christian Counseling and Called to Peace Ministries are two organizations that are known for helping men and women navigate rocky or unsafe relationships.
5. David Powlison, *I'm Exhausted: What to Do When You're Always Tired* (New Growth Press, 2010), 3.
6. David Weber's sprawling Honor Harrington space opera series provides a perfect illustration. In *Echoes of Honor* (Baen Books, 1999), Harrington is held prisoner on the penal moon Hades. Prisoners are largely left unsupervised, an arrangement that works because the moon will not support any plant life that's digestible by human physiology. Guards exercise control by regulating the food rations that are distributed to the prisoners. After a prisoner uprising, guards cut the food supply. The prisoners find that a form of potato will grow and provide just enough nutrients for them to survive, though unfortunately the potatoes also contain toxins that impact the speech centers of their brains. The prisoners eventually escape; however, those who were part of the uprising remain recognizable by their toxin-induced slurred speech. This is a wonderful illustration of how suffering impacts us. However, it's so niche and nerdy that I'll lose most people at "space opera." But since only niche and nerdy people read endnotes, you and I are now coconspirators.

7. C. S. Lewis, *The Four Loves* (Geoffrey Bles, 1960), 77.

Chapter 7: Clouds of Witnesses

1. I would be remiss not to mention that many, many women have served and do serve as caregivers for their chronically ill husbands. Their stories and sacrifices are known by God but have typically not been documented in as much detail. If you're a woman reading this book as a caregiver, I trust you can draw encouragement from the stories that are told here.
2. Ned B. Stonehouse, *J. Gresham Machen: A Biographical Memoir* (Eerdmans, 1954), 220, cited in Fred Zaspel, "Annie Pearce Kinkead (Mrs. B. B.) Warfield, 1852–1915," *Banner of Truth* 595 (2013): 22–26. Machen adds, "I have faint recollections of her walking up and down in front of the house in the early years of my Princeton life, but even that diversion has long been denied her. . . . [She] has seen hardly anyone except Dr. Warfield. But she remained, they say, until the end a very brilliant woman. Dr. Warfield used to read to her during certain definite hours every day. For many, many years he has never been away from her more than about two hours at a time; it has been some ten years since he left Princeton."
3. Robert W. Merry, *President McKinley: Architect of the American Century* (Simon & Schuster, 2017), 42.
4. Merry, 44.
5. Jeffrey G. Mora, "William Jennings Bryan and the 1896 Campaign," *Railroad History* 199 (2008): 72–80.
6. Cited in Betty Boyd Caroli, "Ida McKinley: American First Lady," Encyclopedia Britannica, accessed December 4, 2024, https://www.britannica.com/biography/Ida-McKinley.
7. Allida Black, "Ida Saxton McKinley," The White House, accessed December 4, 2024, https://www.whitehouse.gov/about-the-white-house/first-families/ida-saxton-mckinley/.
8. Caroli, "Ida McKinley."

9. Merry, *President McKinley*, 480.
10. Merry, 481–82.
11. Black, "Ida Saxton McKinley."
12. This quote is a shorter rendering of a longer journal entry. The entry in its fullness drives home the point even more clearly: "It is really true what philosophy tells us, that life must be understood backwards. But with this, one forgets the second proposition, that it must be lived forwards. A proposition which, the more it is subjected to careful thought, the more it ends up concluding precisely that life at any given moment cannot really ever be fully understood; exactly because there is no single moment where time stops completely in order for me to take position [to do this]: going backwards." See Jack Maden, "Kierkegaard: Life Can Only Be Understood Backwards, But It Must Be Lived Forwards," Philosophy Break, October 2023, https://philosophybreak.com/articles/kierkegaard-life-can-only-be-understood-backwards-but-must-be-lived-forwards.
13. I have not talked much in this section about Katelyn's story, as this book primarily focuses on caregivers. Astoundingly, Katelyn came to know Christ as Savior during her stay in the abusive residential facility. This experience transformed her relationship with her suffering. Katelyn writes often on her website, Finding Peace in God's Providence (https://findingpeaceingodsprovidence.wordpress.com). I encourage you to head there and read more. You'll find a woman who reads broadly, thinks deeply, and expresses well the challenges of living with a serious chronic condition.

Chapter 8: The End

1. Neville Longbottom being one of the finest examples of this, of course, as he cuts the head off Nagini the demon-snake in J. K. Rowling's *Harry Potter and the Deathly Hallows*.
2. Thomas R. Schreiner, *The Joy of Hearing: A Theology of the*

Book of Revelation (Crossway, 2021), 156. If you're looking to understand the interplay between the images of the book of Revelation and the way that they're designed to engage your emotions, chapter 6 of Schreiner's book is a helpful resource for further study.
3. Friend, if your loved one does not know the Lord, know that you are pleasing God by taking care of one of his creatures, even if they do not come to know him. Our God gives kind care to those who reject him, and we are to echo his character. Your love and service are beautiful in his sight and in mine, and your love is no less because its object doesn't recognize its Creator.
4. C. S. Lewis, *The Last Battle* (repr., Collier, 1971), chapters 15 and 16.
5. This scene is not in Tolkien's books. Internet chat boards will take you down a dark rabbit hole of discussing why Gandalf would say such a thing given that the elves (and probably he himself) are immortal beings. However, it's a beautiful scene in the movie and a gift to us. (And some of those chat-board commenters need to know their lore better, as elves are immortal unless they are killed in battle, but I digress.) *The Lord of the Rings: The Return of the King*, directed by Peter Jackson (New Line Cinema, 2003).
6. Henry Francis Lyte, "Jesus, I My Cross Have Taken," 1825.

FURTHER RESOURCES

If you've completed this book and are looking for additional help for you and your family, please visit www.couragechristiancounseling.com. This counseling practice offers coaching, counseling, and support groups for individuals and families struggling with chronic pain and illness. You'll find compassionate counselors who understand the contours of a life affected by chronic pain and illness and who are skilled at walking with you in your journey with God, your loved one, and others.

Harris, Greg. *The Cup and the Glory: Lessons on Suffering and the Glory of God*. Kress Christian Publications, 2006.

Kellemen, Bob. *Grief: Walking with Jesus*. 31-Day Devotionals for Life. P&R Publishing, 2018.

Lewis, C. S. *A Grief Observed*. Reprint. HarperCollins, 2001.

Powlison, David. *Safe and Sound: Standing Firm in Spiritual Battles*. New Growth Press, 2019.

Smith, Esther. *A Still and Quiet Mind: Twelve Strategies for Changing Unwanted Thoughts*. P&R Publishing, 2022.

Walton, Jeff and Sarah. *Together Through the Storms: Biblical Encouragements for Your Marriage When Life Hurts*. The Good Book Company, 2020.

Wilson, Andrew and Rachel. *The Life We Never Expected: Hopeful Reflections on the Challenges of Parenting Children with Special Needs*. Crossway, 2016.

From P&R *and the* BIBLICAL COUNSELING COALITION

PAUL TAUTGES

ESTHER SMITH

MEGAN HILL

ELYSE FITZPATRICK

BOB KELLEMEN

ESTHER LIU

In the 31-Day Devotionals for Life series, biblical counselors and Bible teachers guide you through Scripture passages that speak to specific situations or struggles, helping you to apply God's Word to your life in practical ways day after day.

Did you find this book helpful?
Consider leaving a review online.
The author appreciates your feedback!

Or write to P&R at editorial@prpbooks.com
with your comments. We'd love to hear from you.